The Emancipation Proclamation

Abolishing Slavery in the South

Titles in the
Words That Changed History series include:

The Emancipation Proclamation

Abolishing Slavery in the South

by James Tackach

Lucent Books
P.O. Box 289011, San Diego, CA 92198-9011

Library of Congress Cataloging-in-Publication Data

Tackach, James.
  The Emancipation Proclamation / by James Tackach.
    p.   cm. — (Words that changed history)
  Includes bibliographical references (p.   ) and index.
  Summary: Discusses slavery as a cause of the American Civil War and
examines the events surrounding Lincoln's Emancipation Proclamation and
the impact of this declaration on the course of the war and the institution of
slavery.
  ISBN 1-56006-370-X (lib. bdg.)
  1. United States. President (1861–1865 : Lincoln). Emancipation
Proclamation—Juvenile literature.   2. Slaves—Emancipation—United
States—Juvenile literature.   3. Afro-Americans—History—1863–1877—
Juvenile literature.   [1. Emancipation Proclamation.   2. United States—
History—Civil War, 1861–1865.   3. Slavery—History.]   I. Title.
II. Series.
E453.T14   1999
973.7'14—dc21   98-49678
                                                                        CIP
                                                                         AC

Printed in the U.S.A.

Contents

Foreword

"We hold these truths to be self-evident, that all men are created equal, that they are endowed by their Creator with certain unalienable Rights, that among these are Life, Liberty and the pursuit of Happiness." So states one of America's most cherished documents, the Declaration of Independence. These words ripple through time. They represent the thoughts of the Declaration's author, Thomas Jefferson, but at the same time they reflect the attitudes of a nation in which individual rights were trampled by a foreign government. To many of Jefferson's contemporaries, these words characterized a revolutionary philosophy of liberty. Many Americans today still believe the ideas expressed in the Declaration were uniquely American. And while it is true that this document was a product of American ideals and values, its ideas did not spring from an intellectual vacuum. The Enlightenment which had pervaded France and England for years had proffered ideas of individual rights, and Enlightenment scholars drew their notions from historical antecedents tracing back to ancient Greece.

In essence, the Declaration was part of an ongoing historical dialogue concerning the conflict between individual rights and government powers. There is no doubt, however, that it made a palpable impact on its times. For colonists, the Declaration listed their grievances and set out the ideas for which they would stand and fight. These words changed history for Americans. But the Declaration also changed history for other nations; in France, revolutionaries would emulate concepts of self-rule to bring down their own monarchy and draft their own philosophies in a document known as the Declaration of the Rights of Man and of the Citizen. And the historical dialogue continues today in many third world nations.

Lucent Books's Words That Changed History series looks at oral and written documents in light of their historical context and their lasting impact. Some documents, such as the Declaration, spurred people to immediately change society; other documents fostered lasting intellectual debate. For example, Charles Darwin's treatise *On the Origin of Species* did not simply extend the discussion of human origins, it offered a theory of evolution which eventually would cause a schism between some religious and scientific thinkers. The debate still rages as people on both sides reaffirm their intellectual positions, even as new scientific evidence continues to impact the issue.

Students researching famous documents, the time periods in which they were prominent, or the issues they raise will find the books in this series both compelling and useful. Readers will see the chain of events that give rise to historical events. They will understand through the examination of specific documents that ideas or philosophies always have their antecedents, and they will learn how these documents carried on the legacy of influence by affecting people in other places or other times. The format for the series emphasizes these points by devoting chapters to the political or intellectual climate of the times, the values and prejudices of the drafters or speakers, the contents of the document and its impact on its contemporaries, and the manner in which perceptions of the document have changed through time.

In addition to their format, the books in Lucent's Words That Changed History series contain features that enhance understanding. Many primary and secondary source quotes give readers insight into the thoughts of the document's contemporaries as well as those who interpret the document's significance in hindsight. Sidebars interspersed throughout the text offer greater examination of relevant personages or significant events to provide readers with a broader historical context. Footnotes allow readers to verify the credibility of source material. Two bibliographies give students the opportunity to expand their research. And an appendix that includes excerpts as well as full text of original documents give students access to the larger historical picture into which these documents fit.

History is often shaped by words. Oral and written documents concretize the thoughts of a select few, but they often transform the beliefs of an entire era or nation. As Confucius asserted, "Without knowing the force of words, it is impossible to know men." And understanding the power of words reveals a new way of understanding history.

Introduction

The Document That Ended American Slavery

Slavery was America's most grievous sin. For almost 250 years, from 1619 through 1865, slavery remained legal on American soil. During that time period, millions of black Africans and their descendants were held in slavery's bondage with virtually no opportunity to escape from their situation. They labored without pay, lived under wretched conditions, were bought and sold without their consent, and received severe punishments for any act of disobedience to their masters.

Today's student of American history might reasonably ask why slavery persisted so long on the American continent. Since European settlers first began migrating to the so-called New World, America had come to symbolize an escape from the tyranny and oppression that was so common in Europe. Europeans had moved to America to avoid religious persecution and political oppression and to seek a fresh start in a land of new economic opportunity. How could these freedom-seeking new Americans and their descendants tolerate for so long an institution that kept human beings in bondage against their will for their entire lives?

Slavery remained so stubbornly on American soil because it was enormously profitable. From the seventeenth century through the mid–nineteenth century, agriculture was the most important economic activity in America. Before 1860, the overwhelming majority of Americans made their livings through farming, and slaves could play a vital role in an agricultural economy. With little training, they could be taught to plow a field, sow seed and harvest crops, tend animals, and perform other duties essential to the operation of an efficient farm. Particularly in the South, which was more dependent on agriculture for its economic health than the North, slavery was considered a vital institution. By the turn of the nineteenth century, slavery had become illegal in the entire North, but the institution remained in place throughout the South. By 1860, approximately 4 million African Americans worked as slaves on farms and plantations throughout the South; they were important cogs in the South's economy.

Playing such a key role in the South's economy, slavery would not be easily eliminated. For almost 250 years it had remained stubbornly entrenched in American society. Since slavery's inception, abolitionists had condemned it as an immoral institution and called for its removal from American soil—but without much success. Indeed, in 1860, the opponents of slavery seemed to be losing ground in their battle to eradicate the institution; slavery was spreading westward as pioneers began settling the western territories. In 1857, the U.S. Supreme Court, in its *Dred Scott* decision, had ruled that slavery could not be outlawed in U.S. territories and had opened the door for slavery's reintroduction into the Northern states where it had been made illegal.

Surprisingly, the beginning of the undoing of American slavery was a document drafted by President Abraham Lincoln and delivered on January 1, 1863. During the middle of a great civil war, fought between the Northern and Southern states mainly over the issue of slavery, President Lincoln freed most American slaves. Lincoln's Emancipation Proclamation, however, was only a wartime measure specifically designed to weaken the South's ability to continue to wage war. For Lincoln's emancipation document to have any meaning, the North would have to win the Civil War. Lincoln's document would

During the time that slavery was legal in America, blacks endured severe hardships, labored without pay, and lived under miserable conditions.

become moot if the South were able to emerge victorious on the battlefield, secede from the United States, and establish itself as an independent nation with a constitution that protected slavery. Moreover, Lincoln's proclamation would have to be made a part of the U.S. Constitution. The core concept of the Emancipation Proclamation would have to be introduced as an amendment to the Constitution so that it would become part of the fundamental law of the land.

Slavery would finally become illegal in the entire United States with the passage of the Thirteenth Amendment of the Constitution in 1865, almost three years after President Lincoln issued the Emancipation Proclamation. Nonetheless, Lincoln's document set into motion a series of events that would ultimately result in the outlawing of American slavery. The Emancipation Proclamation changed the meaning and purpose of the Civil War, from a war designed to force the rebellious Southern states back into the Union to a war to forever end American slavery. The North's victory in the war spelled the death of slavery. The Thirteenth Amendment made official the idea that Lincoln put forth on January 1, 1863: "All persons held as slaves" in the rebellious Southern states "are, and hence-forward shall be free."[1]

Abraham Lincoln's image adorns this copy of the Emancipation Proclamation, the document that freed most American slaves.

Slavery in America

Slavery took root on the American continent in 1619, when a group of about twenty black Africans taken from their native continent were brought to Jamestown, Virginia, and sold to settlers to work on their plantations. These were the first of a steady stream of Africans brought to America against their will and sold into slavery during the seventeenth century. After 1800, slave importation increased markedly, as a brisk slave trade developed between Africa and America. During the eighteenth century, more than 500,000 Africans were kidnapped on their own continent; brought to America, where they were traded for sugar, molasses, and other American products; and sold in slave markets that had developed in port cities along the eastern coast of North America. Thousands of white Europeans in the eighteenth century had also indentured themselves as servants to American farmers for a period of time to work off the cost of their voyage to America. Unlike the white European immigrants, however, the Africans, as well as their descendants, became slaves for life. Thus began American slavery.

The Spread of Slavery in Colonial America

By 1750, slavery existed in all thirteen of Great Britain's American colonies. In the Northern colonies, however, the institution was only marginally profitable. A Northern slave owner had to house, feed, and clothe his slaves for an entire year, but they could be put to work effectively only during the spring and summer months, when crops were planted, tended, and harvested. The Southern colonies, however, enjoyed a much milder climate and longer growing season. Hence, it became cost effective for Southern growers to maintain slaves to work on their farms and plantations. In Virginia and the Carolinas, slaves worked on large tobacco plantations. In South Carolina and Georgia, slaves grew rice and other crops. (After 1800, cotton would emerge as the South's most important crop.) The economies of Great Britain's Southern colonies became increasingly dependent on slave labor.

Slavery remained legal throughout most of the Northern colonies until the American Revolution. Nonetheless, the number of slaves in the North remained relatively small, so Northern farmers were much less dependent than their Southern counterparts on slave labor. Not

Eli Whitney's Cotton Gin

A machine invented in the late eighteenth century by a New Englander, Eli Whitney, helped sustain slavery's reign throughout the South. In 1793, Whitney, a Massachusetts farmer's son and Yale University graduate, invented a machine to remove seeds from freshly picked cotton balls, a time-consuming process when done by hand. Whitney's cotton gin simply consisted of two rotating cylinders in a box. One cylinder had wire teeth that pulled cotton fibers from the seed, and the second cylinder pulled the seed-free cotton from the wire teeth.

The cotton gin made cotton an extremely profitable crop throughout the South, especially in the Deep South—Georgia, Alabama, and Mississippi. After the invention of the cotton gin, which could be easily duplicated by even the most untrained mechanic, cotton could be processed and sent to market more rapidly. By 1800, cotton became the South's greatest cash crop. Much of the yearly Southern cotton crop was sent to England, where it was processed in British textile mills.

Realizing the great profits in cotton farming, Southern plantation owners rapidly expanded their cotton farms. To work these farms—to perform the laborious tasks of tending and picking cotton in the hot and humid Southern summers—plantation owners sharply increased their slaveholdings. Hence, Southern planters defended slavery on moral grounds—they believed slaves to be inferior to whites—as well as on economic grounds: Slaves had become crucial to the South's economy. If the abolitionists achieved their goal of eliminating American slavery, the South's economy would be ruined.

The cotton gin (short for engine) made cotton farming highly profitable—and heavily dependent on slave labor—in the South.

surprisingly, by the 1770s, the Northern colonies began to eliminate slavery through the passage of emancipation laws that freed slaves immediately or gradually over a period of time. For example, in 1774, the Rhode Island General Assembly prohibited the practice of importing slaves into the colony. The same assembly later decreed that no Rhode Islander could be born into slavery; thus, slavery would end in Rhode Island when the existing slaves passed on.

The American Revolution

By the mid-1770s, the relationship between Great Britain and the American colonies began to deteriorate because of disputes over taxation and other issues. By the summer of 1775, colonial militiamen and British soldiers had clashed in Massachusetts at Lexington, Concord, and Bunker Hill. During the next twelve months, the fighting spread to New York, Canada, and South Carolina. A continental congress had convened twice in Philadelphia to discuss the developing crisis. In June 1776, the members of the Second Continental Congress, seeing no possibility of negotiating with the British government, took the radical step of declaring the American colonies independent from Great Britain. Thomas Jefferson, a brilliant, young congressional delegate from Virginia, was assigned the task of writing the Declaration of Independence.

Thomas Jefferson, the author of the Declaration of Independence.

Jefferson's document boldly and eloquently aligned the colonial cause with lofty principles of liberty and equality. "We hold these truths to be self-evident," wrote Jefferson, "that all men are created equal; that they are endowed by their Creator with certain unalienable rights; that among these are life, liberty, and the pursuit of happiness." Jefferson went on to explain that governments are created to secure and protect these rights and that people have a right to alter or abolish a government that becomes destructive of these basic rights. Then Jefferson listed the various abuses of power committed by England's King George III. The English monarch had dissolved the colonies' legislative bodies. He had kept standing armies in the colonies during peacetime. He had imposed taxes on the colonists without their consent. And he had "waged cruel war against human nature itself, violating its most sacred right of life and liberty in the persons of a distant people who never offended him, captivating them into slavery in another hemisphere, or to incur miserable death in their transportation thither."[2]

But Jefferson's assertion about slavery never made the final draft of the Declaration of Independence that was signed and delivered on July 4, 1776. The slavery clauses were struck from the document when Southern delegates protested. Hence, the unalienable rights of life, liberty, and the pursuit of happiness were not applied to African Americans held in slavery. The war that followed resulted in independence for the American colonies, but American slaves remained in bondage. Ironically, the man who penned the colonies' great Declaration of Independence held slaves throughout his lifetime.

The U.S. Constitution

After a long war, the American colonies achieved their goal: independence from Great Britain. The newly independent American colonies would eventually form the United States of America, a republic held together by a constitution initially comprising seven articles and ten amendments referred to as the Bill of Rights.

Slavery was not a specific issue of discussion and debate at the Philadelphia Convention of 1787, at which the U.S. Constitution was composed. No one proposed the elimination of slavery in the new republic, though early in the convention, George Mason, a delegate from Virginia, alluded to the problem of slavery when he asserted that "We ought to attend to the rights of every class of people" by providing "no less carefully" for the "happiness of the lowest than of the highest order of citizens."[3] But the men at the Philadelphia Convention were men of property, and they ensured that the new government would protect, above all, the rights of property owners, including slave owners.

The new Constitution would not even mention the words *slave* or *slavery*, though it was already clear that rifts had developed between Northern and Southern delegates over issues connected to slavery. For example, Southern delegates wished to include slaves when a state's population was counted to determine the number of delegates the state would be able to send to the House of Representatives, while Northern delegates asserted that slaves could not be counted because they were not considered citizens.

The new Constitution would include the Bill of Rights—a list of guarantees to American citizens, including freedom of religion, freedom of the press, freedom to assemble and protest without government interference, and the right to a fair trial. But the U.S. Constitution, which became the law of the land in 1791, allowed the South to keep its slaves in bondage.

The Three-Fifths Compromise

During the Philadelphia Convention of 1787 that resulted in the composition of the U.S. Constitution, a fierce debate arose over the counting of slaves. The convention delegates decided to create two federal legislative bodies—the Senate, to which each state would send two delegates, and the House of Representatives, whose delegations were determined by the states' populations. The more populous states would be able to send more representatives to the House.

The Southern states wanted to include their slaves in a state's population, but the Northern states objected because slaves were not treated as free citizens. James Wilson, a convention delegate from Pennsylvania, offered a solution to the problem by proposing what became known as the three-fifths compromise. To determine a state's population for representation in the House of Representatives, every five slaves would be counted as three people. Section 2 of Article 1 of the Constitution reads:

> Representatives and direct taxes shall be apportioned among the several States which may be included within this Union, according to their respective numbers, *which shall be determined by adding to the whole number of free persons, including those bound to service for a term of years and excluding Indians not taxed, three-fifths of all other persons.*

The words *slaves* or *slavery* are not used in this article; slaves are merely included among "all other persons."

The three-fifths compromise was one of several compromises reached between North and South over the issue of slavery. By 1860, however, the will to compromise over slavery had waned, and the North and South embarked on a course toward civil war.

Compromises on Slavery

From 1791 to 1820, the North and South lived under an unstable compromise on the issue of slavery: Slavery would remain legal in the South but be prohibited in the North (by 1804, every Northern state had outlawed the institution), and it would not be allowed to spread to any new territories acquired by the United States.

That agreement became threatened in 1819 when the territory of Missouri applied for statehood. At that time, the United States comprised eleven free states and eleven slave states. If Missouri were added as a slave state, it would give the South an advantage in the U.S. Senate, to which each state sent two delegates. After a bitter debate on Missouri statehood, Congress struck a compromise that would admit Missouri as a slave state and Maine as a free state. The Compromise of 1820—also called the Missouri Compromise—also prohibited slavery in U.S. territories north of latitude 36°30′.

That compromise diffused tensions between North and South for a time, but Thomas Jefferson, in retirement at Monticello, his Virginia estate, and paying close attention to the Missouri debate, worried that the latitude line of 36°30′ would become a barrier that would permanently divide his nation into Northern and Southern, antislavery and proslavery, spheres. Jefferson warned against the day when the United States would be split into two separate nations. "A geographical line, coinciding with a marked principle, moral and political, once conceived and held up to the angry passions of men, will never be obliterated; and every new irritation will mark it deeper and deeper,"[4] wrote Jefferson from Monticello to his friend John Holmes.

The Growth of the Abolitionist Movement

Jefferson was correct. The Compromise of 1820 did little to relieve the tensions developing between North and South. The South questioned the right of the federal government to mark an arbitrary line

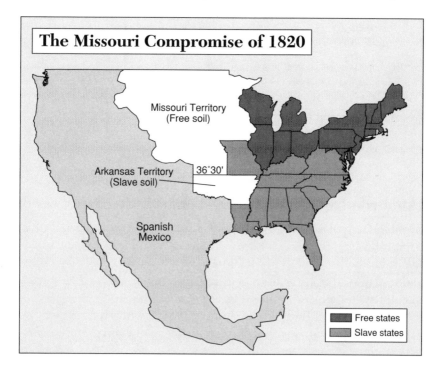

The Missouri Compromise of 1820

Missouri Territory
(Free soil)

Arkansas Territory
(Slave soil)

36°30′

Spanish
Mexico

Free states

Slave states

north of which slavery could not legally exist. Southerners believed that each individual state, not the federal government, should decide whether slavery would be legal within its borders. Northerners protested the Compromise of 1820 because it allowed slavery to spread to the U.S. territories in the west below the latitude line of 36°30′; they had hoped that slavery would be confined to the southern states where it already existed.

Outrage over the possible spread of slavery to the U.S. territories fueled a developing abolitionist movement in the North. Before 1820, the number of American abolitionists—individuals demanding an immediate end to slavery—was small, and they were often labeled radicals or fanatics. After 1820, however, the abolitionist movement gained momentum from a wave of social reforms—religious reform, educational reform, a women's rights movement—that swept the United States. The abolitionist movement gained supporters, and its crusaders became more vocal.

In 1829, David Walker, a slave's son who lived as a free man in Boston, inspired the abolitionist cause when he composed and distributed a pamphlet titled *Walker's Appeal in Four Articles*. The *Appeal* called for an immediate end to American slavery. In fiery language, he warned of certain disaster for the United States if slavery were not eliminated from the land: "Perhaps they will laugh at or make light of this; but I tell you Americans! that unless you speedily alter your course, *you* and your Country are gone!!!!! For God Almighty will tear up the face of the earth!!!"[5] Walker died the year after he published his *Appeal*, but the document was reprinted and widely distributed during the next thirty years.

On January 1, 1831, William Lloyd Garrison, an eloquent abolitionist orator and writer from Massachusetts, published the first edition of an antislavery newspaper titled the *Liberator*. The first edition of the *Liberator* boldly asserted Garrison's purpose:

> I shall strenuously contend for the immediate enfranchisement of our slave population. . . . I am in earnest—I will not equivocate—I will not excuse—I will not retreat a single inch—AND I WILL BE HEARD.[6]

Nat Turner's Revolt

During the summer of 1831, an event occurred that intensified the bitterness developing between the antislavery North and proslavery South. On an August evening, Nat Turner, a Virginia slave, and several comrades staged a twelve-hour bloody rebellion. The slaves escaped from their masters, acquired weapons, and attacked slaveholding farmers in the region. By the time Turner's night of terror

17

The First Abolitionist Document

Opposition to American slavery did not begin after 1820. Abolitionist voices were heard in America as early as the seventeenth century. One of the first Americans to put his opposition to slavery on paper and distribute his views widely was a Massachusetts Puritan named Samuel Sewall.

Sewall was a judge of the Massachusetts Superior Court, and in 1700, he engaged in a debate with another judge who had ruled that a black indentured servant could not be set free, even though the servant's date for release, which had been set in a contract, had arrived. Sewall stated his opinion in the case in a document titled *The Selling of Joseph, a Memorial*, which was published as a pamphlet and distributed throughout Massachusetts Bay Colony. According to Sewall, who relied heavily on the Bible for his reasoning, slavery could be compared to the selling of the biblical Joseph into slavery in Egypt by his jealous brothers. Sewall asserted that slaves were "sons of Adam" who "have equal right unto liberty, and all other outward comforts of life." Sewall believed it "most lamentable to think, how in taking Negroes out of Africa, and selling them here, that which God has joined together men do boldly rend asunder; men from their country, husbands from their wives, parents from their children."

Sewall was among the first Americans to alert the colonies about the evils of slavery. Throughout the eighteenth century, strong abolitionist voices echoed Sewall's views. One of the strongest voices belonged to Benjamin Franklin, who in addressing the Pennsylvania Society for Promoting the Abolition of Slavery correctly warned that slavery was "such an atrocious debasement of human nature, that its very extirpation, if not performed with solicitous care, may sometimes open a source of serious evils."

Samuel Sewall was one of the first to warn Americans about the deplorable nature of slavery.

was over, he and his followers had killed sixty people, including children. Turner fled into the countryside and remained on the run for several weeks, but he was later captured and executed for his actions that night. Before his death, however, Turner narrated his tale to a recorder, who published it as a pamphlet the following year under the title *The Confessions of Nat Turner.* The volume added to the growing body of abolitionist writing being published in the United States.

Southerners blamed William Lloyd Garrison and other vocal abolitionists for Turner's killing spree. Garrison was accused of inciting and supporting slave rebellions through his fiery abolitionist speeches and writings. But these charges did not intimidate Garrison; he responded

Frederick Douglass moved audiences and readers alike with his accounts of slavery's cruelty.

by forming the American Anti-Slavery Society, an organization whose goal was the complete and immediate abolition of American slavery.

In 1841, an ex-slave named Frederick Douglass joined Garrison's crusade. A self-taught reader and writer, Douglass moved audiences with his riveting speeches on the evils of slavery, which he had experienced firsthand. Douglass also became a polished writer; his autobiography, *Narrative of the Life of Frederick Douglass, an American Slave,* published in 1845, sold thousands of copies to a Northern reading audience hungry for details about the lives of slaves.

The Compromise of 1850

Tensions between North and South increased during the late 1840s, when the United States acquired territory comprising New Mexico and California as a result of the Mexican War. Congress staged a bitter debate concerning whether slavery should be allowed in these new territories. The crisis over this issue brought the North and South to the brink of civil war. Once again, however, congressional leaders—Senators Henry Clay of Kentucky, Stephen Douglas of Illinois, and Daniel Webster of Massachusetts—struck a compromise to avoid disaster.

The Compromise of 1850 stipulated that California would be admitted to the United States as a free state; Utah and New Mexico would be established as separate territories, with the question of slavery to be determined by a vote of their citizens; the selling and buying of slaves would become illegal in Washington, D.C.; and a strict fugitive slave law would be enacted to help Southern slave owners recover escaped slaves.

The compromise achieved its immediate goal: It kept the North and South from starting a civil war. But neither side was satisfied with the new compromise. Southerners objected to the admission of a new free state into the Union; now free states outnumbered slave states by sixteen to fifteen. Northerners found the new Fugitive Slave Law to be the most offensive item of the compromise.

The Fugitive Slave Law

The Fugitive Slave Law mandated the hiring of federal commissioners to find and apprehend runaway slaves. These commissioners had the power to require citizens to help capture escaped slaves so that they could be returned to their owners. Abolitionists were outraged. Before the law was passed, slaves who escaped from the South and reached a Northern state would be considered free. Now, the federal commissioners could compel citizens of a Northern state to hunt down fugitive slaves. According to many abolitionists, slavery had now become legal on Northern soil. In an essay titled "Slavery in Massachusetts," Henry David Thoreau, the writer and philosopher from Concord, Massachusetts, maintained that the Fugitive Slave Law "rises not to the level of the head; its natural habitat is in the dirt. It was born and bred, and has its life only in the dust and mire . . . so trample it under foot."[7]

The Fugitive Slave Law became a focus point for the growing number of Americans joining the abolitionist cause. In 1851, Harriet Beecher Stowe, an abolitionist writer living in Maine, reacted to the new law by writing a series of fictional episodes about a pious slave named Uncle Tom for *National Era*, a weekly abolitionist newspaper. For nine months, the paper's readers followed the fortunes of Uncle Tom. After the final episode, Stowe arranged for the weekly pieces to be published as a novel under the title *Uncle Tom's Cabin, or Life Among the Lowly*. To Stowe's surprise, her book became a best-seller in both the United States and Great Britain. The novel describes in sharp and moving detail the horrors of slavery—hard labor without pay, severe beatings for acts of disobedience, the breakup of slave families at the auction block. Stowe's readers wept as they read about the misery of slave life and the tragedy of Stowe's hero, Uncle Tom, who in the novel's final chapters is beaten to death by a cruel master named Simon Legree.

Other writers joined the abolitionist cause: Thoreau, the poet John Greenleaf Whittier, the attorney and orator Wendell Phillips, and women's rights activists Sarah and Angelina Grimké.

135,000 SETS, 270,000 VOLUMES SOLD.

UNCLE TOM'S CABIN

FOR SALE HERE.

AN EDITION FOR THE MILLION, COMPLETE IN 1 Vol., PRICE 37 1-2 CENTS.
"   "   IN GERMAN, IN 1 Vol., PRICE 50 CENTS.
"   "   IN 2 Vols., CLOTH, 6 PLATES, PRICE $1.50.
SUPERB ILLUSTRATED EDITION, IN 1 Vol., WITH 153 ENGRAVINGS,
PRICES FROM $2.50 TO $5.00.

The Greatest Book of the Age.

An advertisement for Harriet Beecher Stowe's book, Uncle Tom's Cabin, *describes the popularity of this antislavery novel.*

The Kansas Crisis

The next battleground between North and South was on the frontier, the Kansas-Nebraska Territory. Since the 1830s, pioneers hungry for more land and wide-open space had been moving westward from Illinois, Iowa, and Missouri to the Kansas-Nebraska Territory. By 1854, this territory was ready for admission to the Union as a state, and the inevitable debate on whether it should be added as a free or slave state began. Senator Stephen Douglas of Illinois proposed that the territory be divided into two states, Kansas and Nebraska, and that the citizens of each state be allowed to decide whether slavery would be

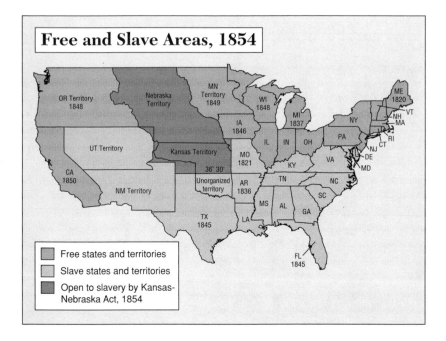

Free and Slave Areas, 1854

OR Territory 1848

Nebraska Territory

MN Territory 1849

WI 1848

ME 1820

VT

NH

MA

NY

MI 1837

UT Territory

Kansas Territory

36° 30'

IA 1846

IL

IN

OH

PA

RI

NJ

CT

CA 1850

NM Territory

Unorganized territory

MO 1821

VA

KY

DE

MD

AR 1836

TN

NC

SC

NM Territory

MS

AL

GA

TX 1845

LA

FL 1845

Free states and territories

Slave states and territories

Open to slavery by Kansas-Nebraska Act, 1854

allowed or prohibited. Douglas's proposal to allow the citizens to vote on whether a state or territory should be free or slave is referred to as popular sovereignty. Southerners supported the idea because it meant that local populations, not the federal government, would decide whether slavery should be legal in an area. Northerners opposed popular sovereignty because it allowed slavery to be further extended.

Douglas's proposal prevailed. After extended and bitter debate, the Kansas-Nebraska Act became law in May 1854. Kansas would be the first of the two territories to decide on the issue of slavery, and both proslavery and antislavery settlers began moving into Kansas for the forthcoming vote on slavery. Not long afterward, violence erupted between the two factions, and Kansas became known as "Bleeding Kansas" as a full-scale civil war broke out.

John Brown's Kansas Crusade

One of the antislavery settlers to migrate to Kansas was an Ohio man named John Brown. Early in 1855, five of Brown's sons moved to Kansas in search of good farmland after a terrible drought in Ohio. When they wrote home to their father about the violence that had erupted in Bleeding Kansas, John Brown headed west to join the battle.

Brown, a Connecticut native, had moved to Ohio as a child with his parents, strong antislavery people who taught young John that slavery was a grievous sin against God. The Brown home became a stop on the Underground Railroad, the secret route by which runaway slaves from the South could cross the Ohio River and escape into the free states or Canada. As he grew into adulthood, Brown became active in the abolitionist cause.

In Kansas, near Pottawatomie Creek, Brown trained a battalion of antislavery settlers to fight in the battle over slavery. On the night of May 23, 1856, Brown led his Pottawatomie Rifles on a nighttime mission to eliminate some of the leaders of the proslavery settlers. During a night of terror, Brown's men stopped at the cabins of three proslavery settlers and brutally murdered five people. In his own mind, however, Brown was no murderer; he had administered just punishment to Kansas men whose goal was to promote the evils of slavery.

When his Kansas work was complete, Brown returned to Ohio and then traveled to the East to solicit funds and followers for a bold new plan to strike again at America's proslavery forces.

John Brown and his followers murdered five people for the abolitionist cause.

The *Dred Scott* Case

Despite the efforts of the abolitionists like William Lloyd Garrison and John Brown, slavery was nowhere in retreat in the United States. The Compromise of 1850, with its notion of popular sovereignty, had permitted slavery's spread to U.S. territories. The Fugitive Slave Law had brought the institution of slavery into the North since runaway slaves remained their masters' property even if they escaped to a free state. The South realized another important gain in its effort to keep slavery flourishing in 1857, when the U.S. Supreme Court ruled on a case involving a slave named Dred Scott.

Dred Scott was a Missouri slave who accompanied his master, John Emerson, to the free state of Illinois, where they lived for a short time. After they moved back to Missouri, Emerson died, and his widow claimed ownership of Scott. At that point, Scott sued for his freedom, claiming that he had become a free man while living in Illinois. Mrs. Emerson maintained that Scott remained her late husband's property even though they had resided for a time in a free state. Scott lost his case in court but appealed the ruling through the federal court system all the way to the Supreme Court, whose opinion on legal matters is binding on all parties. In 1857, the Supreme Court addressed Scott's case, and seven of the Court's nine justices ruled against Scott, meaning that he would remain a slave, the property of Mrs. Emerson.

Roger B. Taney, the chief justice of the Supreme Court, composed and issued the Court's ruling in the case that became known as *Dred Scott*. According to Taney, Scott was not a citizen of the United States. In Taney's mind, the British government, before the American Revolution, regarded black Africans as "beings of an inferior order, and altogether unfit to associate with the white race, either in social or political relations." The Declaration of Independence, which separated the colonies from Great Britain, indeed asserted that "all men are created equal," but according to Taney, "it is too clear for dispute, that the enslaved African race were not intended to be included, and formed no part of the people who framed and adopted this declaration." The Constitution identified the people living in the thirteen independent states as citizens of those states and of the newly formed republic, but Taney asserted that blacks "were not even in the minds of the framers of the Constitution when they were conferring special rights and privileges upon the citizens in every other part of the Union."[8] Hence, Dred Scott was not a U.S. citizen and possessed no constitutional rights.

Dred Scott sued for his freedom after his master died.

Rather than a citizen of the United States, Dred Scott was and remained a piece of property belonging to Emerson and later to his widow, even though Emerson had taken Scott to a free state. Wrote Chief Justice Taney:

> The right of property in a slave is distinctly and expressly affirmed in the Constitution. The right to traffic in it, like an ordinary article of merchandise and property, was guaranteed to the citizens of the United States, in every State that might desire it. . . . And the Government in express terms is pledged to protect it in all future time, if the slave escapes from the owner.[9]

In other words, Scott, according to Taney, was no different from the horse or wagon that Emerson brought to Illinois. When Emerson brought his property to a free state, he retained ownership of it, even if his "property" was a human being.

Chief Justice Taney's decision in the case of *Dred Scott* offered one more troubling ruling. Taney concluded that Congress had no right to outlaw slavery in any state or territory; that was a decision left solely to the inhabitants of each state or territory. Hence, Taney's decision rendered the Compromise of 1820 unconstitutional because it had outlawed slavery in U.S. territories above the latitude mark of 36°30′.

Reaction to the *Dred Scott* Decision

Southerners applauded the Supreme Court's decision. They had always considered their slaves to be private property, and they had always opposed the idea that the federal government could restrict slavery in any region of the United States.

Antislavery Northerners condemned Chief Justice Taney and his Court's ruling. Most abolitionists embraced the notion that the Declaration of Independence's assertion that "all men are created equal" applied to both white and black Americans. Abolitionists considered African Americans as American citizens who inherited all the rights and liberties guaranteed by the Constitution.

Abolitionists feared the long-term implications of the *Dred Scott* decision. If the federal government had no right to regulate slavery, then the institution could spread across the entire American continent, to every territory acquired by the United States. Furthermore, if one slave owner, John Emerson, could bring one slave, Dred Scott, into a free state and retain possession of that slave as a piece of personal property, what would prevent a slave owner from bringing one hundred slaves into a free state and settling there permanently? Could slavery be introduced to states where it was already illegal?

One Northerner particularly concerned about the long-term impact of *Dred Scott* was an Illinois politician, a member of the newly formed Republican Party, Abraham Lincoln. Lincoln, like his fellow Republicans, vehemently opposed any extension of slavery, and he feared that the *Dred Scott* ruling would allow the institution to overspread the entire country. In a speech delivered in Columbus, Ohio, on September 16, 1859, Lincoln warned of a follow-up to the *Dred Scott* decision, a "second" *Dred Scott* decision "making slavery lawful in all the States." [10]

John Brown's Raid

Another antislavery Northerner outraged by the *Dred Scott* decision was John Brown, the abolitionist who had waged war against the proslavery forces in Bleeding Kansas. Brown, like many abolitionists, sensed that the "Slave Power," the slaveholding Southern planters and the politicians who supported them, was gaining momentum in its effort to extend slavery across the United States. Brown was tiring of listening to preachers and politicians condemn slavery in speeches and sermons. He reasoned that only bold action could rid America of the evil institution.

Early in 1858, Brown began implementing a plan that he had formulated during his days in Kansas. He planned to ignite a massive slave revolt, a bloody rebellion during which armed slaves would attack and slay their masters, free themselves forever, and rid America of slavery. Brown began to recruit men and solicit funds at abolitionist meetings throughout the North. During the summer of 1859, Brown and several of his followers rented a farmhouse in Maryland near the banks of the Potomac River.

Brown's plan was directed at Harpers Ferry, a small town on the Virginia side of the Potomac River that held the U.S. weapons arsenal. Weapons were made in a Harpers Ferry gun factory and stored in nearby warehouses. Brown reasoned that if he could capture the arsenal, which was not heavily defended, he could arm hundreds of slaves on nearby farms and plantations. Those slaves could liberate themselves and attack other plantations, and the rebellion would spread through Virginia and Maryland and eventually throughout the entire South.

Harpers Ferry, West Virginia, where John Brown attempted to start a rebellion against slavery in October 1859.

On the evening of October 16, 1859, Brown and his twenty-one crusaders stole into Harpers Ferry, cut telegraph lines, apprehended the sentries who guarded the weapons warehouses, and took control of the town. He also sent several men to nearby plantations to liberate the slaves and urge them to join his rebellion.

But early the next morning, Brown's grand plan began to unravel. A railroad train entered and left Harpers Ferry, and the conductor spread the news of Brown's raid. Soon nearby Virginia militiamen were marching toward Harpers Ferry. They shot and captured several of Brown's men and trapped the rest in a firehouse in town. The next day, a battalion of U.S. Marines, under the command of Colonel Robert E. Lee, arrived in Harpers Ferry by order of President James Buchanan. Lee's troops rushed the firehouse where Brown was trapped, killing several of Brown's men and capturing Brown. His revolution had lasted less than forty-eight hours.

The Trial of John Brown

Brown was indicted for treason and murder. The Virginia authorities who held him hoped for a quick trial and an immediate execution. But Brown did not go quietly to the gallows. His trial made the front pages of newspapers across the United States. His statements to the court were printed in full, and he became the subject of fiery editorials, speeches, and sermons. Southerners condemned Brown as a traitor and murderer, a Satan who had designed to ruin the entire Southern way of life. To abolitionists, however, Brown was a hero, a saint, a man who had gone beyond speeches and manifestos in his effort to destroy American slavery. Henry David Thoreau, for example, saluted Brown as a man who "gave his life to the cause of the oppressed."[11]

Brown was found guilty and hanged on December 2, 1859, but he was not quickly forgotten. On the day of his death, church bells throughout the North tolled for a fallen martyr, and abolitionist ministers, politicians, and orators eulogized Brown in fiery speeches. In Northern churches and at antislavery rallies, abolitionists began singing a song called "John Brown's Body," whose chorus intoned, "John Brown's body lies a-moulderin' in the grave, / But his soul is marching on!"

On a Course Toward War

John Brown's rebellion put the United States on a course toward civil war. In Congress, Southern representatives accused their Northern counterparts of masterminding Brown's raid and thereby igniting a war to eradicate slavery and destroy the South. Southerners wondered

The lyrics to the song "John Brown's Body."

JOHN BROWN SONG!

John Brown's body lies a mouldering in the grave,
John Brown's body lies a mouldering in the grave,
John Brown's body lies a mouldering in the grave,
His soul's marching on!

CHORUS.

Glory Hally, Hallelujah! Glory Hally Hallelujah! Glory Hally Hallelujah!
His soul's marching on!

He's gone to be a soldier in the army of the Lord,
He's gone, &c
He's gone, &c.
His soul's marching on!

CHORUS.

Glory Hally, Hallelujah! &c.
His soul's marching on!

John Brown's knapsack is strapped upon his back—
John Brown's, &c.
John Brown's, &c.
His soul's marching on!

CHORUS.

Glory Hally, Hallelujah! &c.
His soul's marching on!

His pet lambs will meet him on the way—
His pet lambs, &c.
His pet lambs, &c.
They go marching on!

CHORUS.

Glory Hally, Hallelujah! &c.
They go marching on!

They will hang Jeff Davis to a tree!
They will hang, &c.
They will hang, &c.
As they march along?

CHORUS.

Glory, Hally, Hallelujah! &c.
As they march along!

Now, three rousing cheers for the Union!
Now, &c.
Now, &c.
As we are marching on!

CHORUS.

Glory Hally, Hallelujah! Glory Hally, Hallelujah! Glory, Hally, Hallelujah!
Hip, Hip, Hip, Hip, Hurrah!

☞Published at No. 256 Main Street,
CHARLESTOWN, MASS.

28

how many other abolitionists like Brown were planning some bloody revolt. During one session of the House of Representatives a few days after Brown's death, a Mississippi congressman attacked Representative Thaddeus Stevens of Pennsylvania, an abolitionist, with a bowie knife. A murder was avoided only because Stevens's Republican colleagues were able to break up the scuffle. Congressmen began carrying guns and knives in the halls of Congress. The days of compromises over slavery were over.

With 1860 a presidential election year, the future of American slavery and the fate of the Union might be in the hands of the man who would ascend to the presidency after the November elections.

The Draftsman and His Document

The 1860 presidential election would prove to be one of the most critical in U.S. history. The fate of American slavery—and, in turn, the fate of the Union—was at stake. At the Democratic Party's political convention during the spring of 1860, the delegates split over the issue of slavery. Northern Democrats nominated Stephen Douglas, a senator from Illinois, as their presidential candidate, and Southern Democrats nominated John Breckinridge of Kentucky, President James Buchanan's vice president. In Chicago, the Republicans united behind Abraham Lincoln of Illinois, a lawyer and former member of the House of Representatives, and one of the nation's most articulate commentators on the issue of American slavery.

Young Man Lincoln

Abraham Lincoln was born in a log cabin in Kentucky in 1809. A pioneer family, the Lincolns moved frequently. During his childhood, Abraham received no more than a year of formal education, but like many other Americans born before public schooling became available, he taught himself to read and write. As a young man, Lincoln moved to New Salem, Illinois, where he held a variety of jobs, studied law, and later won a seat in the Illinois legislature. After obtaining his license to practice law, Lincoln set up a profitable private law practice, with much of his business coming from the fast-expanding American railroad companies.

But Lincoln was as interested in American politics as he was in law, and he became a politician. He was elected to the House of Representatives in 1847 and served one two-year term. Though he focused mainly on his law practice for the next several years, Lincoln remained interested in the political issues that occupied Americans in the mid–nineteenth century, particularly the growing debate over slavery.

Lincoln on Slavery

Early in his life, Lincoln formed a strong distaste for the institution of slavery. Slavery violated everything for which Lincoln stood. He had been born into a poor pioneer family that made its livelihood tilling the soil; his parents were uneducated. Yet through personal determination, Lincoln had risen to the social rank of prosperous lawyer. Lincoln believed that all Americans should have the opportunity to enhance their lives as he had enhanced his own. Slavery negated that possibility. The overwhelming majority of slaves were slaves for life, with no opportunity to rise above their station and improve their lives or the lives of their children. Moreover, Lincoln believed that slavery violated the principle, articulated by Thomas Jefferson in the Declaration of Independence, that all men are created equal.

An experience as a young man solidified Lincoln's misgivings about slavery. He and his close friend Joshua Speed were traveling south from Springfield, Illinois, on a Mississippi riverboat. On board was a man from the Deep South who had purchased twelve slaves at an auction in Kentucky. In a letter to Speed's sister, Mary, Lincoln described the unpleasant scene in detail:

They were chained six and six together. A small iron clevis was around the left wrist of each, and this fastened to the main chain by a shorter one at a convenient distance from, the others; so that the negroes were strung together like so many fish upon a trot-line. In this condition they were being separated forever from the scenes of their childhood, their friends, their fathers and mothers, and brothers and sisters, and many of them, from their wives and children, and going into perpetual slavery.[12]

Yet despite his personal distaste for slavery, Lincoln did not consider himself an abolitionist. He believed that the federal government had no

Even though slavery violated everything for which he stood, Lincoln did not think of himself as an abolitionist.

right to interfere with slavery in the South where it already existed. When he served as a member of the Illinois legislature, Lincoln signed a petition with several other Illinois assemblymen opposing a measure calling for the abolition of slavery throughout the nation. Nonetheless, Lincoln strongly opposed the extension of slavery to the U.S. territories.

Lincoln endorsed what he called a "middle ground" on the slavery issue: Slavery should be allowed to continue in the states where it already existed, but it should not be allowed to spread to other states or territories. In taking that position, Lincoln aligned himself with Kentucky senator Henry Clay, whom Lincoln greatly admired. Lincoln hoped that if slavery were not allowed to spread elsewhere in the United States, it would eventually die out in the South. Lincoln also maintained that the Founding Fathers of the American republic expected slavery to eventually disappear from the United States.

Like many other antislavery Americans, Clay included, Lincoln also believed that free African Americans should have the right to relocate to Africa. Early in his political career, Lincoln supported the creation of a colony in Africa to which free African Americans could be sent.

The Colonization Plan

Before the Civil War, many Americans believed that one resolution to the national problems stemming from the institution of slavery was to gradually free American slaves and send them to reside in a colony in Africa. To that end, the American Colonization Society was established in 1816. The organization acquired land on the west coast of Africa that became known as Liberia. Between 1822 and the Civil War, about fifteen thousand free African Americans migrated to Liberia and made the land their permanent home.

Many Northerners actively supported the colonization plan. They feared that if American slaves were ever emancipated, they would move to the North and take jobs from white laborers by offering to work for lower wages than those paid to whites. Some Northerners thought slavery morally wrong but still wished to see the United States develop into a whites-only nation, so the colonization plan also appealed to those people.

African Americans like Frederick Douglass opposed the colonization concept. Douglass believed that blacks born in America, including slaves, were Americans, not Africans, and they had the right to remain in the United States and enjoy all the privileges of American citizenship. Abraham Lincoln initially supported colonization. After he delivered the Emancipation Proclamation, however, African Americans began enlisting in the Union army to fight for their freedom; 186,000 black troops would eventually serve in the conflict. Seeing blacks fight to defend the Union prompted Lincoln to abandon any colonization plan.

Campaigning for the Senate

In 1858, Lincoln seized on the opportunity to spread his beliefs on the slavery issue to the American public. Lincoln was named by the newly formed Republican Party to oppose Stephen Douglas, a Democrat, in Douglas's effort to retain his seat in the U.S. Senate for a third term. The Senate campaign against Douglas allowed Lincoln to spell out to the voters of Illinois his beliefs on slavery and other issues of national importance. And not only were the citizens of Illinois keying in on this Senate race, but the rest of the nation, sensing the importance of the Illinois campaign, was tuning in as well.

Lincoln opposed Douglas's concept of popular sovereignty, because it allowed for slavery to spread to U.S. territories. After Douglas forged the Kansas-Nebraska Act and ushered it through the Senate, Lincoln, delivering an address in Peoria, Illinois, criticized the act, calling it "wrong; wrong in its direct effect, letting slavery into Kansas and Nebraska—and wrong in its prospective principle, allowing it to spread to every other part of the wide world, where men can be found inclined to take it." [13]

Lincoln laid the foundation for his debate with Douglas in a speech in Springfield, Illinois, on June 16, 1858, an address that became known as "The House Divided" speech. Quoting the New Testament, Lincoln asserted:

> "A house divided against itself cannot stand."
>
> I believe this government cannot endure, permanently half *slave* and half *free*. I do not expect the Union to be *dissolved*— I do not expect the house to *fall*—but I *do* expect it will cease to be divided. It will become *all* one thing, or *all* the other. [14]

Lincoln went on to comment on the Supreme Court's recent decision in the *Dred Scott* case, expressing his fear that a future Court ruling would prevent any state from excluding slavery. He also predicted that Douglas's notion of popular sovereignty would reinstate the African slave trade (which by 1858 had been made illegal) and allow slavery to spread throughout the United States.

The Lincoln-Douglas Debates

During their campaign for the Illinois Senate seat, Lincoln and Douglas engaged in a series of seven debates on slavery and other issues of national importance. The debates were well attended, and transcripts or excerpts of the comments by each candidate were published in newspapers throughout the United States.

In the debates, Lincoln repeated his positions on slavery that he had been developing during the previous several years: that the institution

In the Lincoln-Douglas debates, Lincoln declared that slavery was "a moral, a social and a political wrong."

of slavery did not square with the affirmations of equality in the Declaration of Independence, that Congress ought to prevent the spread of slavery into U.S. territories, that the Supreme Court's decision on *Dred Scott* opened the door for legalizing slavery throughout the North, and that his aim was not to abolish slavery where it already legally existed. Lincoln also battled Douglas on moral grounds. In the first debate, Lincoln asserted that proslavery Southerners, and the politicians who supported them, like Douglas, wished to "blow out the moral lights around us; they must penetrate the human soul, and eradicate there the love of liberty; and then and not till then, could they perpetuate slavery in this country." Likewise, in the sixth debate, Lincoln declared that the Republicans judged slavery as "a moral, a social and a political wrong."[15]

Douglas tried to push Lincoln into asserting that black Americans deserved exactly the same social and political rights that whites enjoyed, an opinion unpopular even among Americans who opposed slavery. Lincoln tried to negate Douglas's argument on that point, explaining in the first debate, "I have no purpose to introduce political and social equality between the white and black races. . . . I, as well as Judge Douglas, am in favor of the race to which I belong, having the superior position." Lincoln reiterated that point in the fourth debate, stating that he had never supported the idea of "making voters and jurors of negroes, nor qualifying them to hold office, nor to intermarry with white people. . . . I as much as any other man am in

The Republican Party

Early in 1854, the Whig Party fell into disunion over the issue of slavery. Shortly thereafter, Whigs pledged to restricting or abolishing slavery began meeting across the North to discuss their concerns. At one meeting on March 20, 1854, in Ripon, Wisconsin, the delegates decided to form a new party whose mission it was to restrict the spread of American slavery. The new party was called the Republican Party and later became affectionately nicknamed "The Grand Old Party."

The Republicans included rabid abolitionists like Charles Sumner of Massachusetts and William Seward of New York. Southerners labeled men like Sumner and Seward "Black Republicans" because of their focus on the issue of slavery. The Republicans also included moderate politicians like Abraham Lincoln of Illinois, who did not promote the abolition of slavery but did speak forcefully against its spread to other states and territories.

The Republican Party put forth its first presidential candidate in the election of 1856. Republican Charles Frémont of California finished second in the electoral vote to James Buchanan, 174-114. In 1860, the Republicans united behind Lincoln and ran a strong antislavery campaign, while the Democrats fell into bickering and disunion over slavery. Hence, Lincoln won the election.

Charles Sumner and other zealous abolitionists were called "Black Republicans" by Southerners for their intense hatred of slavery.

favor of having the superior position assigned to the white race."[16] Lincoln also explained that he was not in favor of citizenship for black Americans.

These statements by Lincoln troubled some of the abolitionists of his time and continue to trouble today's historians and biographers of Lincoln. Did Lincoln really believe that African Americans were, as a race, inferior to whites? Some historians and biographers, taking these comments on race at face value, believe that Lincoln was a racist. Others, however, suggest that Lincoln's comments must be taken in their original context—as part of a political debate, an effort to win an election. To affirm that blacks and whites were equal and should be treated equally would have been political suicide for Lincoln in 1858. As Lincoln biographer Stephen B. Oates argues, "Such allegations [by Douglas] forced Lincoln to take a stand. It was either that or risk political ruin in white-supremacist Illinois."[17]

Stephen Douglas (pictured) would challenge Lincoln once again, this time for the White House.

Despite Lincoln's efforts during the debates, he lost his election to Douglas. Nonetheless, his political career was far from over. During the campaign, Lincoln had built his reputation as one of the Republican Party's most eloquent spokesmen, a definite candidate for high public office in the future.

Lincoln's Campaign for the White House

In 1860, when the Republicans met at their convention in Chicago to choose their candidate for the forthcoming November election, Lincoln's name was in the minds of many of the convention delegates. After his loss to Douglas two years earlier in the Senate campaign, Lincoln had continued to address the issues of the day in his speeches and writings. He had become a nationally known and respected public figure.

Lincoln's main Republican opponent was William Seward, a firm abolitionist. The convention delegates, sensing that Lincoln's moderate middle ground on slavery might attract voters who were not abolitionists, threw their support to Lincoln, and he emerged from the convention as the Republican Party's standard bearer in the 1860 presidential campaign.

The Democrats' convention in Charleston, South Carolina, broke up after a bitter debate on the slavery issue. Northern Democrats reconvened in Baltimore and nominated Lincoln's political opponent of the 1858 Senate race, Stephen Douglas. Southern Democrats chose Vice President John Breckinridge. Thus, the Democratic vote in the November election would be split, with some Democrats voting for Douglas and some for Breckinridge. In addition, the members of the Whig Party, which had all but disintegrated in 1854 after the Republican Party was formed, established the Constitutional Union Party and nominated John Bell of Tennessee as their presidential candidate. Thus, the Republicans united behind Lincoln, while his opponents divided themselves among three other candidates.

In those days, the presidential candidates did not actively participate in their campaigns; they remained in the background while prominent members of the party carried the campaign to the voters. Lincoln observed this tradition, but Douglas hit the campaign trail. He tried to paint Lincoln as an extremist, one of the so-called Black Republicans who wished to abolish slavery and ruin the South's economy or force the South to secede from the Union and drive the nation toward civil war. Douglas painted himself as the moderate candidate who could hold the nation together during these difficult times.

Predictably, however, Lincoln's opposition fragmented, and Lincoln carried the election. Lincoln won only 40 percent of the popular vote, but he carried 180 electoral votes to 72 for Breckinridge, 39 for Bell, and only 12 for Douglas. Lincoln won

Lincoln won the 1860 presidential election over Douglas, Bell, and Breckinridge (pictured).

the electoral votes of all Northern states, while the Southern states divided their votes among his three opponents. In March 1861, Lincoln would become the nation's sixteenth president.

The South Secedes from the Union

Soon after the election, Douglas's prediction about the disintegration of the Union came true. In December, the South Carolina legislature voted 169-0 to withdraw from the United States. In January, Mississippi followed South Carolina's lead, as did Florida, Alabama, Georgia, Louisiana, and, in February, Texas. Representatives from these states met in Montgomery, Alabama, and formed the Confederate States of America, with Jefferson Davis as president. Most of the South was now in open rebellion against the Lincoln presidency, even though he had not yet taken office. Four slave states—Maryland, Delaware, Kentucky, and Missouri—however, remained loyal to the Union.

Lincoln maintained that no state could withdraw from the United States, that in adopting the Constitution, each individual state had made itself a permanent part of the Union. He considered secession an act of anarchy that must be dealt with quickly. But not yet in office, Lincoln could do little to reverse the action taken by the seceders. President Buchanan spoke strongly against secession, but he was a lame duck president in his final weeks in office; the South would not listen to his pleas for unity.

Lincoln did not want a civil war to break out over the issue of secession; he hoped that the South could be brought back into the Union through careful negotiations. "Now, in my view of the present aspect of affairs, there is no need of bloodshed and war," he said in a speech in Philadelphia ten days before taking office. "There is no necessity for it. I am not in favor of such a course, and I may say in advance, there will be no blood shed unless it be forced upon the Government. The Government will not use force unless force is used against it."[18]

Again in his First Inaugural Address, delivered on March 4, 1861, after he took the oath of office for the presidency, Lincoln tried to

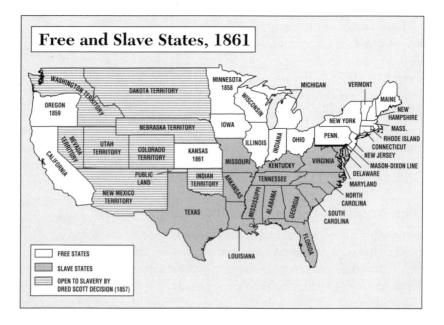

Free and Slave States, 1861

FREE STATES
SLAVE STATES
OPEN TO SLAVERY BY
DRED SCOTT DECISION (1857)

reach out to the rebellious South. He promised that he had no intention of trying to abolish slavery in the states where it existed. He quoted one of his earlier speeches, saying, "I have no purpose, directly or indirectly, to interfere with the institution of slavery in the States where it exists. I believe I have no lawful right to do so, and I have no inclination to do so." He also reminded the rebellious South that "the Union of these States is perpetual" and that any attempt to leave the Union was "legally void." Moreover, Lincoln asserted that "the central idea of secession, is the essence of anarchy." He concluded his long speech with poetic and conciliatory words of friendship:

> I am loth to close. We are not enemies, but friends. We must not be enemies. Though passion may have strained, it must not break our bonds of affection. The mystic chords of memory, stretching from every battle-field, and patriot grave, to every living heart and hearthstone, all over this broad land, will yet swell the chorus of the Union, when again touched, as surely they will be, by the better angels of our nature.[19]

The Coming of War

But even as Lincoln delivered those conciliatory words to the South, a crisis was developing in South Carolina that could ignite a war. After South Carolina withdrew from the Union, it demanded the evacuation of Fort Sumter, a U.S. garrison situated in Charleston harbor. If the U.S. government would not release the fortress, South Carolina militiamen would attack it. The morning after he took office, Lincoln received a dispatch from the fort's commander, Major Robert Anderson. He needed reinforcements and supplies to hold the garrison against attack.

Major Anderson's request presented a problem for Lincoln. If Lincoln sent a fleet of ships to reinforce and resupply Fort Sumter, that might be considered an act of war; the supply fleet might be fired upon by the large guns defending Charleston harbor, guns that were now in the hands of the South Carolina militia. If Lincoln did not reinforce Anderson, the South Carolinians would easily overpower the fort. If Lincoln decided to abandon Fort Sumter, the entire North would read it as an act of weakness by the new president. Editorials in Northern newspapers urged Lincoln to reinforce the gallant group of soldiers defending Fort Sumter, but General Winfield Scott, Lincoln's top military adviser, recommended evacuating the garrison.

Lincoln decided not to abandon Fort Sumter. He ordered unarmed ships to bring food and supplies to the fort; he hoped that the South Carolinians would not fire on unarmed boats that carried no

Fort Sumter on April 14, 1861, after its surrender to Confederate troops. The lightly defended garrison had undergone a day and a half of artillery fire from Charleston shore batteries.

men or material for war. But President Jefferson Davis ordered an attack on the fort before the supply ships arrived. At dawn on April 12, batteries in Charleston opened fire on the lightly defended fort. After a day and a half of bombardment, Major Anderson surrendered his fortress.

The war had come. The day after Fort Sumter's surrender, Lincoln called for the enlistment of seventy-five thousand troops to put down the Southern rebellion. Within weeks, Virginia, Arkansas, North Carolina, and Tennessee also withdrew from the Union, giving the Confederacy eleven states.

The South's Early Victories

The North demanded swift and decisive retaliation for the Confederate attack on Fort Sumter. During the spring and early summer of 1861, Brigadier General Irvin McDowell, commander of the Union army in Washington, began amassing a large force to invade the South. His target was a large Rebel army in Manassas, Virginia, only twenty-five miles from Washington. McDowell hoped to deal the South a quick blow by destroying this army; then he would press on to Richmond, the capital of the Confederacy. With Northern troops occupying the South's capital city, the Confederacy's will to fight a war would be broken.

On July 16, General McDowell began moving his thirty-five thousand troops southward. Five days later, the two armies clashed at Bull Run Creek near the Manassas railroad junction. At first, McDowell's attack seemed successful, as his troops pushed the Rebels backward.

But the Southerners rallied behind General Thomas Jackson, later nicknamed "Stonewall Jackson" for his determined stance against the Yankee troops at Manassas. Southern reinforcements arrived by train at a key moment in the battle and drove the Northern troops back. The Yankees retreated, then fled the field and headed back toward Washington.

The Battle of Bull Run shocked Lincoln and the North. The North's best army had been soundly defeated; moreover, the total casualties in the battle—thirty-five hundred men on both sides—made both the North and South realize that this conflict might turn into a long and bloody civil war. The Southern rebellion would not be put down in ninety days as most northerners predicted. Lincoln now called for 400,000 additional volunteers to fight in this civil war.

No more major battles took place in 1861, but the following spring and summer, major engagements occurred in

Brigadier General Irvin McDowell led the attack on the Rebel army in Manassas, Virginia.

The Battle of Bull Run Creek near Manassas was a shocking defeat for the North.

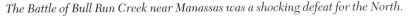

both Virginia and the Mississippi valley. A spring offensive mounted by Northern armies along the coast of Virginia—later called the Peninsular Campaign—ended in disaster for the North. In April in Shiloh, Tennessee, Northern and Southern armies clashed in a bloody stalemate that resulted in twenty-three thousand casualties. In August, the two sides fought again at Bull Run Creek. In none of these engagements could the North deliver a decisive victory to break the Rebel resolve.

The Battle of Antietam

In September 1862, the commander of the Confederate army, General Robert E. Lee of Virginia, decided on a bold plan to invade Northern soil. Lee had gained confidence from his battlefield victories of the previous years, and he reasoned that he could invade the Northern states of Maryland and Pennsylvania to put pressure on Lincoln to call a truce. Lee moved his fifty-thousand-man army from Manassas on September 3 and marched into Maryland uninhibited. Meanwhile a Federal force of seventy thousand troops, under the command of General George McClellan, moved from Washington to meet Lee. On the morning of September 17, the two armies met in farm fields along Antietam Creek, near the small town of Sharpsburg, Maryland.

Armies of the North and South clash along Antietam Creek in Maryland. Twenty-two thousand men from both sides fell in a single day, the bloodiest day of the entire Civil War.

The Battle of Antietam was one of the bloodiest of the Civil War. The two armies battled from dawn through sundown, with neither side gaining any substantial advantage. At the end of this day of terrible fighting, the Union had incurred twelve thousand casualties and the South ten thousand—the bloodiest single day of combat in the entire Civil War. After the battle, Lee withdrew his troops from Yankee territory and returned to Virginia, and McClellan regrouped to fight another day.

Lincoln and the North considered the Battle of Antietam a victory, even though it was essentially a stalemate. The North claimed that its army had halted Lee's invasion of Northern soil. Coming after so many Southern victories, McClellan's checking of Lee at Sharpsburg seemed like an event for the North to celebrate, even though McClellan had lost so many men and Lincoln later sharply criticized his commanding general for not pursuing Lee's battered army back into Virginia. More importantly, this so-called victory at Antietam Creek allowed Lincoln to put forward a plan that he had been considering since the opening months of the war.

A Plan to Free the Slaves

Initially, for Lincoln, this civil war was not being fought over the issue of slavery; it was a war to reverse the South's withdrawal from the Union. Lincoln made it clear that if the rebellious Southern states returned to the Union, they would return with the institution of slavery still in place. As the war entered its second year, however, the abolitionists in Congress began pressing the president to free the slaves. Freeing the slaves would cripple the South's ability to wage war because the labor performed by slaves would have to be performed by men who might otherwise enlist in the Confederate army.

Senator Charles Sumner of Massachusetts offered Lincoln another reason for freeing the slaves. Great Britain was considering recognizing the Confederacy as an independent nation and perhaps supporting the South in its effort to free itself from the Union. England had been siding with the South because British textile mills were dependent on the South's cotton. Since the war, the amount of cotton exported to Great Britain had significantly decreased, mainly because Lincoln had ordered a naval blockade of the South, preventing its trade ships from sailing overseas. But Sumner tried to convince Lincoln that if America's civil war became a war over slavery rather than a conflict over saving the Union, the British would not recognize or aid the South, because the British were vehemently against slavery.

Frederick Douglass, the ex-slave and abolitionist leader, urged Lincoln to free the slaves in an editorial in his abolitionist newspaper:

The Negro is the key of the situation—the pivot upon which the whole rebellion turns. Teach the rebels and traitors that the price they are to pay for the attempt to abolish this Government must be the abolition of slavery.[20]

Indeed, many slaves were already achieving their freedom. With the South's manpower enlisted in the army instead of overseeing farms and plantations, it was relatively easy for slaves, especially those living in states that bordered the North, to escape from bondage. Thousands did, and many offered their services to the Union army. During the early part of the war, blacks were prohibited from joining the Union army as soldiers, but Federal generals accepted the offers of runaway slaves to work for the North's cause. Escaped slaves were put to work in a variety of army jobs. General Ulysses S. Grant, the commander of the Union army in the Mississippi River region, wrote in a letter to his family that he was using escaped slaves as "teamsters, hospital attendants, company cooks and so forth, thus saving soldiers to carry the musket."[21]

In March and again in July 1862, Congress passed slave confiscation acts. The first act prohibited military personnel from returning runaway slaves to their owners. The second act, which Lincoln opposed, freed all of the slaves of owners who supported the Southern rebellion.

Lincoln Acts

Lincoln had already long been considering what his abolitionist advisers and abolitionist congressmen were urging. He hinted of his plan in a letter to Horace Greeley, founder and editor of the *New York Tribune:*

My paramount object in this struggle *is* to save the Union, and is *not* either to save or to destroy slavery. If I could save the Union without freeing *any* slave I would do it, and if I could save it by freeing *all* the slaves I would do it; and if I could save it by freeing some and leaving others alone I would also do that.[22]

The letter does reiterate Lincoln's claim that the war was being waged over the South's secession, not over its slaves. But the letter to Greeley also suggests that Lincoln was ready to free the slaves as a means to achieve his goal of restoring the Union.

Lincoln's secretary of state, William Seward, urged Lincoln not to take any action regarding the slaves until the North achieved a decisive victory on the battlefield; if the North were losing the war, rea-

Early Acts of Emancipation

Although the Emancipation Proclamation often earns credit for freeing American slaves, Abraham Lincoln's executive order was actually only one of a series of emancipatory acts passed during the Civil War. In July 1861, just a few months after the war began, the United States Congress passed a bill confiscating slaves who had been compelled by their owners to engage in any work that would directly aid the South's rebellion. This act freed slaves who worked in ammunitions factories or as cooks, quartermasters, or laborers for the South's armies. The following March, Congress enacted a wartime measure forbidding military personnel from returning fugitive slaves to their owners; soldiers who disobeyed this law would be subject to court martial.

In July 1862, Congress anticipated Lincoln's Emancipation Proclamation by passing a bill that freed all slaves whose owners supported the South's cause. Under this act, only the slaves of pro-Union owners could remain in slavery once the Union was restored. Lincoln's Emancipation Proclamation, announced in September 1862 and issued officially on January 1, 1863, rubber-stamped what Congress had already attempted the previous summer.

soned Seward, a grand gesture to free the slaves would have little effect. On September 22, 1862, five days after the Battle of Antietam, Lincoln acted on behalf of the slaves, issuing his Preliminary Emancipation Proclamation. That document announced that, as of January 1, 1863, slaves held in the states in rebellion against the Union "shall be then, thenceforward, and forever free,"[23] and that the U.S. government and its military would do nothing to repress that freedom. This proclamation warned the South that states in rebellion against the North would lose their legal right to hold slaves after January 1. In the same document, Lincoln offered to put forward a plan that would allow slave owners in states loyal to the Union to give up their slaves and receive financial compensation from the federal government for doing so.

Lincoln's proclamation was applauded by abolitionists but criticized by Northerners who did not wish to see the war turn into a war over slavery. Northern Democrats accused Lincoln of issuing an order that violated the Constitution. In the November elections, the Democratic Party scored some gains by campaigning against Lincoln's proclamation. Some political observers suggested that Lincoln might withdraw his order to free the slaves because of the criticism and the accompanying political fallout.

The Emancipation Proclamation

Lincoln remained true to his word. On January 1, 1863, Lincoln issued a Final Emancipation Proclamation. The document lacked the poetic language that Lincoln so often showed in his speeches and writings; the Emancipation Proclamation is a legal document that features clear, straightforward language.

Lincoln begins by establishing his legal authority for issuing such a document. He issues the proclamation "by virtue of the power in me vested as Commander-in-Chief, of the Army and Navy of the United States in time of actual armed rebellion against authority and government of the United States, and as a fit and necessary war measure for suppressing said rebellion."[24] In other words, Lincoln was not freeing American slaves for moral or philosophical reasons; he was freeing the slaves as an act of war, to deprive the rebellious South of one of its important assets. Lincoln then names the states in rebellion, making it clear that the slaves in states loyal to the Union—Maryland, Delaware, Kentucky, and Missouri—were still in bondage.

Lincoln reads the first draft of the Preliminary Emancipation Proclamation to members of his cabinet on July 22, 1862. Six months later Lincoln issued the final version despite the threat of criticism and political fallout.

In clear and precise language, Lincoln goes on to pronounce the slaves in the rebellious states free: "I do order and declare that all persons held as slaves within said designated States, and parts of States, are, and henceforward shall be free." Lincoln adds that the freed slaves ought to "abstain from all violence, unless in self-defense" and recommends that "they labor faithfully for reasonable wages." Lincoln includes one more controversial point concerning the freed slaves in his Emancipation Proclamation: "And I further declare and make known that such persons of suitable conditions, will be received into the armed service of the United States to garrison forts, positions, stations, and other places, and to man vessels of all sorts in said service."[25] Hence, Lincoln agreed with an argument pressed by Frederick Douglass and other abolitionists—that African Americans should be recruited to fight in the Union army.

Lincoln concluded his proclamation by asking for God's blessing on his momentous decision: "And upon this act, sincerely believed to be an act of justice, warranted by the Constitution, upon military necessity, I invoke the considerate judgment of mankind, and the gracious favor of Almighty God."[26]

The Public Reaction

Predictably, the South condemned Lincoln for his Emancipation Proclamation. To proslavery Southerners, Lincoln was no better than John Brown, who had, in 1859, attempted to ignite a bloody war to free the South's slaves. President Jefferson Davis of the Confederacy considered Lincoln's action "the most execrable measure recorded in the history of guilty man."[27] Lincoln's Emancipation Proclamation steeled the South's resolve to win the Civil War. To lose the war would mean an end to Southern slavery and the ruination of the South's economy.

Abolitionists and African American civil rights activists like Frederick Douglass applauded both Lincoln's freeing of the slaves and his decision to allow blacks into the U.S. army. In their minds, Lincoln had changed the war's objective, from a war to restore the Union to a war to end American slavery. His Emancipation Proclamation raised the stakes of the Civil War. If the South lost, it could no longer limp back into the Union with slavery intact. If the South prevailed in the conflict, slavery would remain a part of Southern life. If the North triumphed, however, the South would be forced back into the Union to form a nation forevermore free from slavery.

3 The War to Free the Slaves

President Abraham Lincoln's Emancipation Proclamation, delivered on January 1, 1863, changed the purpose of the Civil War. The conflict had begun, in 1861, as a war to restore the Union, an effort to negate the votes of secession taken by eleven Southern states to protest Lincoln's election and to respond to the battle at Fort Sumter. When Lincoln freed the slaves in the rebellious states, however, his war aims changed. He had come to realize that peace between North and South could never be permanently established if the South returned to the Union with its 4 million slaves; with slavery still in place, the North and South, even if reunited, would continue bickering and eventually go to war again. As Lincoln had said in 1858 in his famous "House Divided" speech, his country could not permanently stand half slave and half free; it would eventually become all one or all the other. Now he was determined that it be reunited all free, with slavery forever forbidden. For the next two years, Lincoln, with his words and actions, would attempt to convince his country to embrace this goal.

Northern Troops Protest

The entire North did not immediately espouse Lincoln's change of purpose. Northern Democrats criticized Lincoln's Emancipation Proclamation and the subsequent shift in the goal of the war. Those loudly critical of Lincoln became known as copperheads because of their venomous attacks on the Lincoln administration's policies. One particularly vocal copperhead, Congressman Clement Vallandigham of Ohio, urged Northern soldiers to desert so that Lincoln could no longer wage his war to free the slaves. Vallandigham was ultimately arrested by the army and tried and convicted of treason.

But some Union troops listened to Vallandigham and other copperheads who urged them to abandon Lincoln's war. In one regiment from Lincoln's own state, the 128th Illinois, all but thirty-five men deserted, refusing to fight in a war to free the slaves. Moreover, the war was already two years old, with no victory in sight, and many soldiers, whether or not they supported Lincoln's Emancipation Proclamation, were ill, tired of fighting, and anxious to return home. Southern troops also deserted in large numbers.

Southern Victories

Two Southern battlefield victories, one at the end of 1862 and one in the spring of 1863, did little to lift the sagging spirits of Northern troops. On December 13, 1862, Yankee and Rebel troops clashed at Fredericksburg, a town on Virginia's Rappahannock River midway between Washington and Richmond. Union troops attacked a high ground outside of Fredericksburg called Marye's Heights that was solidly defended by General Robert E. Lee's infantry and artillery. Union Major General Ambrose Burnside sent wave after wave of Yankee regiments up the heights into the Rebel gunfire. Burnside's Yankees were cut to pieces; they never came within a hundred yards of the Confederate defenses. After a day of terrible fighting, dead and wounded Yankee troops were strewn on Marye's Heights. Some of the wounded men, left untended by overworked medical crews, froze and bled to death on the cold December night. Burnside lost 12,600 men, while Lee lost only 5,000.

The bitter Union defeat at Fredericksburg made some Northerners read Lincoln's forthcoming Emancipation Proclamation as an empty and meaningless document. If the North could not win on the battlefield, how would Lincoln's gesture of emancipation ever gain any force? Lincoln himself was depressed by the results from Fredericksburg. He began to wonder whether the Union could ever win this horrible war.

Union troops charge Marye's Heights at Fredericksburg, Virginia. Wave after wave of soldiers under the command of General Ambrose Burnside were cut down by Confederate General Robert E. Lee's defenses.

In April 1863, another Union defeat, at Chancellorsville, Virginia, further depressed Northern spirits. Having wintered in Virginia after the crushing December defeat at Fredericksburg, the Federal army regrouped and was reinforced for another campaign against General Lee's troops in the spring. The two armies clashed again at Fredericksburg and nearby Chancellorsville. Badly outnumbered, Lee nonetheless engineered a staggering defeat on the Union army. With only 60,000 men, Lee, commanding a series of brilliant offensive maneuvers and surprise attacks, sent a Union army of 130,000 men reeling into an embarrassing retreat.

Lee Invades the North

Encouraged by his stunning victory at Chancellorsville, Lee decided that it was time for another invasion of the North. His earlier attempt to take the war to Northern soil ended when his army was checked at Antietam Creek, but his recent battlefield successes suggested that the Army of the Potomac, the main Northern army in the Virginia theater, was vulnerable. Lincoln had tried a handful of generals to command the Army of the Potomac, but none was successful. Lee con-

The New York Draft Riots

During the summer of 1863, President Lincoln issued a draft call to recruit men for the Union army. Lincoln's order was not popular with all citizens of the North. On July 13, while the names of draftees were being drawn at a draft office on Manhattan's east side, an angry mob attacked the facility. They ransacked the office, then proceeded to set the building on fire. Looting and rioting ensued.

For three days the rioting continued. Black citizens were the main targets of the violence. Rioters did not wish to see white citizens drafted into an army that was fighting to liberate the slaves. A black church, a black orphanage, and black boardinghouses were burned; black citizens were beaten and lynched. Police and militiamen called to the scene were attacked by rioters. Eventually, hundreds of weary troops from Gettysburg arrived on the scene and gained control of the streets. During the melee, 105 people were killed.

The draft riots, which also occurred less extensively in other Northern cities, showed that Lincoln's war to save the Union and end slavery was not supported by the entire population of the North.

vinced President Jefferson Davis of the Confederacy that a campaign into the North might result in a fatal blow to Lincoln's war effort.

In early June, Lee began to move his seventy-three-thousand-man Army of Northern Virginia out of its camp near Fredericksburg. He marched his troops north through the Blue Ridge Mountains into Maryland, a Union state. Unimpeded, Lee pressed his army into Pennsylvania. His target was the city of Harrisburg, where Lee could ready his troops for a siege of Philadelphia. If Lee could capture and hold a major Northern city like Philadelphia, he believed that he could bring Lincoln to the peace table. To stop Lee at that point, Lincoln would have to recognize the Confederacy's independence.

A large Union army consisting of 110,000 men under the command of Major General George Meade began to move northward with Lee. Meade kept his troops between Lee's army and Washington, D.C., to dissuade Lee from attacking the North's capital. As Lee moved north, the two opposing armies moved closer to each other. On July 1, they made contact near the small town

Major General George Meade led Union forces to victory at Gettysburg.

of Gettysburg when Lee's men marched toward town to capture a shoe factory. After their long march from Virginia, many of Lee's men needed new shoes. Early in the morning on July 1, Yankee and Rebel battalions skirmished west of Gettysburg.

Victory at Gettysburg

Later on July 1, the two huge armies moved into position for a major confrontation. After the early fighting, Meade's men retreated southward to the high ground outside of the town of Gettysburg. They posted themselves on Cemetery Ridge, forcing Lee to fight uphill if he wanted to dislodge his enemy army. Lee's troops moved into town and positioned themselves east and southwest of town in the woods along Seminary Ridge.

On the second day of the battle, Lee ordered a major offensive on the Union left flank by troops under the command of Lieutenant General James Longstreet. After several hours of fierce fighting

51

around two hills named Little Round Top and Big Round Top, the Yankees held their position, mainly because of a heroic defensive stand taken by the 20th Maine Regiment. Longstreet's advance was thwarted, and the Federals also repulsed advances on their right flank.

After two days of fierce fighting, neither side had gained a significant advantage. Lee had come close to victory, but the Union army had held its ground. Both sides had endured staggering casualties. Unwilling to settle for a stalemate, Lee planned a major offensive on the Union position for the next day.

Early in the afternoon of July 3, Lee ordered a two-hour artillery bombardment on the center of the Union position on Cemetery Ridge. He hoped to soften the Union defenses for an all-out attack. At 3:00 P.M., Lee ordered thirteen thousand troops under the command of Major General George Pickett to advance on the Union center. His men marched out of their position in the woods across an open field. Sensing Pickett's attack, General Meade had massed his men on the center of his line. When Pickett's men were within firing range, hundreds of artillery pieces and thousands of rifles fired at once, blasting huge holes in the Rebel lines. The Confederates kept charging, but the Union guns cut them down before they could reach the Union position.

The Yankee line held. Confederates who reached it were quickly killed or captured in savage hand-to-hand fighting. Badly damaged, Pickett's men withdrew, limping across the open field over which they had just optimistically advanced. Half of Pickett's thirteen thousand men had been killed or wounded. The Union army had suffered staggering losses as well, but it was still firmly in position at the end of that day of terrible fighting.

Lee knew that he was beaten. In the epic three-day battle he had lost twenty-eight thousand men, while the Federal army had suffered twenty-three thousand casualties. Lee called off his invasion of the North. He retreated back into Virginia while the North celebrated a major victory. On the same day, July 3, General Ulysses Grant captured the important city of Vicksburg, Mississippi, on the Mississippi River, giving the North a double victory. Lee's advance in the East had been stopped, and Grant had gained control of the Mississippi River. These two great Northern victories changed the tide of the war.

The Enlistment of Black Troops

The two victories at Gettysburg and Vicksburg during the summer of 1863 uplifted Northern spirits. Further encouragement for the Northern cause that summer came from a new source of manpower: African American troops began to enlist in the Union army.

Lincoln's Emancipation Proclamation had announced a new War Department policy to allow blacks to enlist in the Union army and fight to end slavery. Encouraged by African American leaders like Frederick Douglass, thousands of young African American men, free Northern men and escaped slaves alike, joined the Union ranks during the next few months. At first, black soldiers performed only menial jobs—loading ammunition wagons, guarding camps and bridges, digging graves—but by the summer of 1863, they were ready for combat. In June, a black regiment saw action at a skirmish at Lilliken's Bend, Louisiana, and gave a good account of itself.

Two weeks after the great victory at Gettysburg, a black Union regiment, the 54th Massachusetts, led the Union charge on Fort Wagner in South Carolina. The attack against a strongly fortified Confederate position was not well planned, but the regiment impressed the entire North with its valor. Unflinchingly, the black troops, commanded by a white officer, Colonel Robert Gould Shaw of Massachusetts, marched into Confederate cannon and gunfire. The 54th Massachusetts suffered 40 percent casualties in the offensive, but no man failed in his duty, dispelling the notions of those who thought that black troops could not be disciplined and would not demonstrate courage on the battlefield.

The Emancipation Proclamation allowed blacks to enlist in the Union army and join in the fight against slavery. African American soldiers were at first assigned menial tasks but soon proved themselves in combat.

Before the end of the war, more than 185,000 black soldiers would serve in the Union army. The influx of fresh troops, at a crucial moment in the war, helped put the North on the road toward victory.

The 54th Massachusetts

Among the first regiments of African American soldiers formed during the Civil War was the 54th Massachusetts, which saw action in the failed Union offensive on Fort Wagner, South Carolina, on July 18, 1863. The six hundred men of the 54th Massachusetts led the charge on the South Carolina battery. Forty percent of the regiment were killed or wounded in the attack, including its white commanding officer, Colonel Robert Gould Shaw, the son of prominent Boston abolitionists.

Both the Union and the Confederates generally sent the bodies of slain enemy officers back to their lines after the battle so that they could be returned home for proper burial. The Confederates holding Fort Wagner decided not to release Colonel Shaw's remains because he commanded black soldiers. When asked about returning Shaw's body, a Rebel officer reportedly stated that the grave diggers "buried him with his niggers." The Confederates considered that an insult, but Shaw's father interpreted the act differently. "The poor, benighted wretches thought they were heaping indignities upon his dead body," Mr. Shaw reported to the press, "but the act recoils upon them. . . . They buried him with his brave, devoted followers who fell dead over him and around him. . . . We can imagine no holier place than that in which he is . . . nor wish him better company—what a bodyguard he has!"

The courage exhibited by African American soldiers at Fort Wagner caught President Lincoln's attention. A month after the battle, Lincoln, in a letter to Democratic critics, defended his decision to allow black men to enlist in the Federal army. Lincoln stated that "the emancipation policy, and the use of colored troops, constitute the heaviest blow yet dealt to the rebellion." Lincoln believed that when the war was won "there will be some black men who can remember that, with silent tongue, and clenched teeth, and steady eye, and well-poised bayonet, they have helped mankind on to this great consummation."

The 54th Massachusetts became the subject of the 1989 feature film *Glory*, starring Matthew Broderick as Colonel Shaw and Morgan Freeman and Denzel Washington as two of his soldiers.

Lincoln's Changing Attitude on Race

For Lincoln, the Civil War had begun as an endeavor to force the rebellious Southern states back into the Union. Though Lincoln personally opposed slavery, its abolition was not his most immediate war aim. Midway through the terrible conflict, however, he realized that freeing the slaves was a necessary war measure. First, Lincoln knew that it would deprive the South of much-needed manpower. Second, he fully realized that the Union could never be permanently restored if it remained half slave and half free. Hence, he issued the Emancipation Proclamation.

Lincoln's decision to change the war from a war over secession to a war over slavery also signaled a change in his attitude regarding issues of race. When Lincoln had run for the Senate in 1858, Senator Stephen Douglas had pressured Lincoln into stating that African Americans were inferior to whites, that they did not deserve the same rights of citizenship enjoyed by white Americans. During the harsh crucible of war, however, Lincoln discarded that concept. After realizing that abolishing slavery was the key to ending the conflict between North and South, and after recruiting black soldiers in the war and seeing them perform nobly on the field of battle, Lincoln finally fully comprehended that his nation must completely solve its racial problems. That would mean doing more than eliminating all forms of American slavery; it would mean extending the guarantees of liberty and equality articulated by Thomas Jefferson in the Declaration of Independence to all Americans, black and white.

A Wartime Order

Evidence of Lincoln's changing attitude appears in a wartime executive order delivered by Lincoln on July 30, 1863, less than a month after the Battle of Gettysburg. Lincoln had heard upsetting reports that Confederate officers had ordered captured African American troops to be sent into slavery or, worse, to be summarily executed. Lincoln was profoundly disturbed to hear these reports. He believed that all captives, regardless of race, should be treated as prisoners of war. In response to these reports, Lincoln issued an order of retaliation concerning the capture of soldiers on the battlefield.

Lincoln opened his order by asserting the fundamental equality of all citizens, including soldiers:

> It is the duty of every government to give protection to its citizens, of whatever class, color, or condition, and especially to those who are duly organized as soldiers in the public service. The laws of nations and the usages and customs of war as carried

on by civilized powers, permit no distinction as to color in the treatment of prisoners of war as public enemies. To sell or enslave any captured person, on account of his color, and for no offense against the laws of war, is a relapse into barbarism and a crime against the civilization of the age.

Lincoln then informed the South that if its commanders executed any captured Union soldier, black or white, he would order a captured Confederate soldier executed in return. If any captured Union soldier were sent into slavery, "a rebel soldier shall be placed at hard labor on the public works and continued at such labor until the other shall be released and receive the treatment due a prisoner of war."[28]

This order subtly reveals Lincoln's evolving attitude on race. He asserts that a government is duty-bound to protect all of its citizens, regardless of race, and he endorses the concept of equal treatment under law for all human beings. By asserting the dignity of all soldiers, Lincoln was making an affirmation about the basic equality of all human beings.

Lincoln at Gettysburg

Lincoln would make one of his most eloquent statements about race on the Gettysburg battlefield several months after the battle was fought. The occasion was the dedication of a national cemetery at Gettysburg to provide a proper burial place to those who died there during that fierce three-day battle in July. Lincoln was invited to offer a few words at the dedication ceremony, scheduled for November 19, 1863.

Myths surround Lincoln's Gettysburg Address—one being that he hurriedly wrote his speech on the back of an envelope while on the train to Gettysburg. Actually, Lincoln, a slow and careful writer, worked hard on the address. He wished to express his nation's appreciation for the men who fought and fell at Gettysburg. More importantly, perhaps, he wished to put into words the purpose of the terrible civil war in which his nation had been engaged for almost three years; he wished to give meaning to the awful conflict, to explain to Americans that the war was being fought for some worthwhile cause.

Lincoln was not the keynote speaker at Gettysburg. That honor belonged to Edward Everett, a nationally known orator. According to the ceremony's program, Lincoln was scheduled to offer only "Dedicatory Remarks" after Everett's oration. After Everett's speech, which

Lincoln gives his address at Gettysburg. Although it lasted only about three minutes, Lincoln had worked hard to put into words the purpose and meaning of the war.

lasted about two hours, Lincoln approached the podium and used about three minutes to convey to his audience, and to the nation, his newly realized meaning of the war.

The Gettysburg Address

Lincoln began by reminding his audience that only eighty-seven years ago America's Founding Fathers had established a new nation, "conceived in Liberty, and dedicated to the proposition that all men are created equal." He explained that that proposition was now being tested "in a great civil war"; he noted the purpose of the day's ceremony—to dedicate "a final resting place for those who here gave their lives that that nation might live." Lincoln assured his listeners that it was "altogether fitting and proper that we should do this."[29]

Then Lincoln went on to examine the Battle of Gettysburg "in a larger sense." He expressed his appreciation for what the men who died did at Gettysburg, and he urged his audience "to be dedicated here to the unfinished work which they who fought here have thus far so nobly advanced," that "from these honored dead we take increased devotion to that cause for which they gave the last full measure of devotion." He asserted that the dead at Gettysburg "shall not have died in vain" because their nation, under God, "shall have a new birth of

Lincoln the Writer

Though he received very little formal education, Abraham Lincoln is generally recognized as the American president most skilled in crafting speeches and written documents. His great speeches—the Gettysburg Address, the Second Inaugural Address—are among the best and most studied in American history.

From his study of law, Lincoln learned to use words and language precisely. From his reading of the Bible and the works of William Shakespeare, Lincoln developed a prose style frequently marked by the lyricism and imagery associated with the best poetry. In the Gettysburg Address, for example, he uses the imagery of birth, death, and rebirth to convey to his listeners what was happening to their country. The nation, "conceived" in liberty, was being tested by a great civil war during which brave men "gave their lives" with the hope that the nation might experience a "new birth of freedom."

Lincoln's favorite rhetorical device was repetition, particularly repetitions of three. At Gettysburg he asserted that "we can not dedicate—we can not consecrate—we can not hallow" the sacred ground consecrated by those who fell in battle. In the same speech, he hoped that his nation's government "of the people, by the people, for the people shall not perish from the earth." Similarly, in his Second Inaugural Address, Lincoln urged the country "to finish the work we are in; to bind up the nation's wounds; to care for him who shall have borne the battle, and for his widow, and his orphan."

Lincoln also frequently used alliteration, the repetition of consonant sounds to start words, as in his First Inaugural Address when he speaks of the "mystic chords of memory" stretching from patriot battlefields and graves. Similarly, during a campaign speech in New Haven, Connecticut, in 1860, Lincoln urged those committed to the idea of preserving the Union to "dare to do our duty, as we understand it."

The Emancipation Proclamation was a legal document that called for clear, straightforward prose. In other writings and speeches, however, Lincoln was capable of complex imagery, poetic language, and lyrical sentence patterns.

freedom." He concluded with his hope that this American government "of the people, by the people, for the people, shall not perish from the earth."[30]

Lincoln never used the words *slave* or *slavery;* he did not speak specifically of racial inequalities. But he clearly informed Americans of the meaning of their terrible war. It was a war about equality, a war that would determine whether every American would have equal opportunity—to work, to earn and save money, to live in peace, to be treated equally under the law. The Gettysburg Address was a logical extension of the Emancipation Proclamation. After Lincoln had freed the slaves and thereby changed the purpose of the war, he saw the struggle as a fundamental testing of the Declaration of Independence's assertion that all men are created equal. The soldiers at Gettysburg died to defend that proposition, not merely to restore the Union. As historian Garry Wills has stated, "In the crucible of the occasion, Lincoln distilled the meaning of the war, of the nation's purpose, of the remaining task, in a statement that is straightforward yet magical."[31]

The Tide Changes

The Union victories at Gettysburg and Vicksburg did not end the war. The South fought on stubbornly. But the tide surely had changed. Early in 1864, Lincoln appointed General Ulysses Grant commander of the entire Northern army. Grant had essentially won the war in the Mississippi region, and he would come east to destroy General Lee's army.

In May and June 1864, Grant and Lee fought a series of brutal battles in Virginia that lasted six weeks. Grant could not completely destroy Lee, but he imposed staggering losses, and the Confederate army became short of men. In June, Grant commenced a long siege

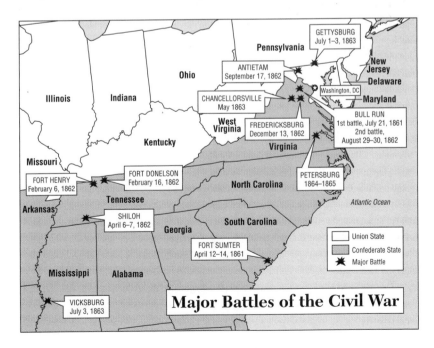

Major Battles of the Civil War

In early 1864, General Ulysses Grant was appointed commander of the entire Northern army.

of Petersburg, a key city southeast of Richmond, the Confederate capital. Meanwhile, one of Grant's most talented lieutenants, General William Sherman, began an offensive in Tennessee with the goal of fighting his way to the strategic Southern city of Atlanta, Georgia. Sherman's campaign, later called "Sherman's March to Sea," inflicted heavy damages on the Confederate army and the Southern landscape, thereby breaking the South's resolve.

The Election of 1864

In the middle of the terrible conflict, Lincoln had to run for reelection. His term in office would end in March 1865, and the election was set for November 1864. Some of Lincoln's advisers urged him, as commander-in-chief of the armed forces, to order a suspension of the election until the war ended. But Lincoln was determined that the proper democratic procedures take place, despite the war. As he asserted in a postelection address, "We cannot have free government without elections; and if the rebellion could force us to forgo, or postpone a national election, it might fairly claim to have already conquered and ruined us."[32]

The Democrats nominated George McClellan, the Union general who had stopped Lee's advance at Antietam Creek two years earlier. Lincoln had dismissed McClellan from command of the Army of the Potomac because the general had not pursued Lee after the Battle of Antietam. The Democratic platform called for a truce with the South. McClellan did not energetically endorse that platform, but during the campaign he was sharply critical of Lincoln's handling of the war.

Fortunately for Lincoln, by the time the election came, the Northern armies had gained some victories on the battlefield. Sensing a change in the tide of the war, the American voters handed Lincoln a landslide victory. With the rebellious Southern states not voting, Lincoln received 55 percent of the popular vote and 212 electoral votes to McClellan's 21. As 1864 came to a close, Lincoln prepared for another four years in office.

The Second Inaugural Address

On March 4, 1865, Lincoln took his second oath of office. As is customary, he followed the oath with an inaugural address. Lincoln used this opportunity, as he had at the Gettysburg cemetery dedication, to explain to his fellow Americans the meaning and purpose of the dreadful war that had occupied their nation for almost four years. This Second Inaugural Address is much shorter than the speech delivered after his first inauguration, when he pleaded with the rebellious South to rejoin the Union and avoid a civil war.

Lincoln opened his address by reminding his audience of the situation four years earlier, when he was attempting to save the Union, while "insurgent agents were in the city seeking to *destroy* it without war—seeking to dissolve the Union, and divide effects, by negotiation. Both parties deprecated war; but one of them would *make* war rather than let the nation survive; and the other would *accept* war rather than let it perish. And the war came." Lincoln goes on to explain the reason for the conflict:

> One eighth of the whole population were colored slaves. . . . These slaves constituted a peculiar and powerful interest. All knew that this interest was, somehow, the cause of the war. To

strengthen, perpetuate, and extend this interest was the object for which the insurgents would rend the Union, even by war; while the government claimed no right to do more than to restrict the territorial enlargement of it.[33]

Here Lincoln clearly identifies slavery, not secession, as the essential cause of the war. Secession and the accompanying war were the inevitable effects of the nation's unresolvable debate over slavery.

God's Vengeance

Lincoln notes in his Second Inaugural Address that both North and South pray to the same God for victory on the battlefield, though he doubts that a just God could help a nation of slaveholders: "It may seem strange that any men should dare to ask a just God's assistance in wringing their bread from the sweat of other men's faces." Lincoln then identifies American slavery as "one of those offenses which, in the providence of God, must needs come, but which, having continued through His appointed time, He now will to remove, and that He gives to both North and South, this terrible war, as the woe due to those by whom the offense came." Lincoln prays that "this scourge of

During his Second Inaugural Address, Lincoln (center, at podium) described slavery as a terrible sin for which an angry God sent the Civil War as due punishment.

war may speedily pass away." Yet he fears that the war will continue "until all the wealth piled by the bond-man's two hundred and fifty years of unrequited toil shall be sunk, and until every drop of blood drawn with the lash, shall be paid by another drawn with the sword."[34]

Thus, Lincoln identifies slavery as a terrible sin for which God has sent a terrible war as due punishment. The sin was not the bickering between North and South that led to disunion; the sin was slavery itself, committed by the South but tolerated by the North to protect the Union. Now, as the thousands of dead on Civil War battlefields attest, both sides must pay in blood for committing this sin, until every drop of blood caused by the slave owner's whip is repaid with a drop of blood on the battlefield.

Lincoln concludes his address with words of healing, an olive branch of peace held out to the rebellious South:

> With malice toward none; with charity for all, with firmness in the right, as God gives us to see the right, let us strive on to finish the work we are in; to bind up the nation's wounds; to care for him who shall have borne the battle, and for his widow, and his orphan—to do all which may achieve and cherish a just, and a lasting peace, among ourselves, and with all nations.[35]

Lincoln's Second Inaugural Address provides further explanation and justification for his Emancipation Proclamation. He informs his nation that he had to free the slaves. In Lincoln's view, as long as slave owners continued to demand from their slaves labor without pay, as long as they pushed their slaves by drawing blood with the whip, God would continue to require that blood be shed on the battlefield. Lincoln realized that he could not stop the bloodshed of war without ending the sin of slavery. After almost four years of death and carnage, Lincoln had firmly grasped the war's meaning.

CHAPTER 4 From Proclamation to Amendment

President Abraham Lincoln set several important goals for his second term of office. First, and most important, he wished to conclude the war as quickly as possible. Once the war was over, Lincoln hoped to reconstruct his fragmented country, to bring the rebellious South back into the Union and to broker a lasting peace between the two warring regions of his country. To accomplish that goal, Lincoln knew that he would have to rid the nation of slavery forever. On January 1, 1863, in his Emancipation Proclamation, he had freed the slaves only in the states in rebellion. Lincoln fully realized that slavery's permanent abolition would have to be guaranteed in the U.S. Constitution so that it would vanish forever from American soil.

These were ambitious goals, but Lincoln was prepared for the hard work ahead. He had ushered his nation through the most difficult period in its history; he had held his country together during a bitter civil war, which was nearing its end as Lincoln began his second term in office. His reelection in 1864 proved that the people were behind him in his effort. Unfortunately, Lincoln would have only a very short time—barely six weeks—to accomplish these goals.

Winning the War

By the time Lincoln took his oath of office to begin his second term, the North's armies had gained a significant advantage on the battlefield. General William Sherman had taken the key cities of Atlanta and Savannah, Georgia, and he was pressing northward into South Carolina. In February, he had reached Columbia, South Carolina, the capital city of the first state that seceded from the Union in 1860. Sherman continued marching northward into North Carolina toward Virginia.

Meanwhile, General Ulysses Grant continued his yearlong siege of Petersburg, Virginia, an important railroad junction only twenty miles from Richmond, the Confederate capital. The battle for Petersburg had begun the previous spring, when Grant had pressed his ninety-thousand-man army on the city hoping for a quick victory. But General Robert E. Lee's seasoned troops mounted a staunch defense of the key Southern city, and Grant began a long siege, posting his troops in long trenches outside and nearly surrounding the city. As the winter of 1864–1865 came, the Rebel soldiers and citizens of Petersburg suffered shortages of food, fuel, and clothing.

By the end of March, Lee knew that he could no longer defend Petersburg. On April 2, he removed his troops and moved northward across the Appomattox River, and Yankee soldiers occupied Petersburg. Lee's Army of Northern Virginia and another Confederate force battling General Sherman in North Carolina were the last significant Rebel armies between the North and complete victory. Sensing defeat, thousands of Confederate soldiers deserted and headed for home, hoping to bring neglected farms back into shape for spring planting. After Petersburg fell, the remaining Confederate soldiers defending Richmond abandoned that city, and President Jefferson

After four years of bloodshed, General Robert E. Lee (pictured) surrendered his forces to General Ulysses Grant at Appomattox Courthouse.

Davis and his advisers fled Richmond as well. Yankee troops soon occupied the Confederate capital. The Southern cause was all but lost.

Lee Surrenders at Appomattox

After occupying Petersburg, Grant's troops pursued Lee. The two armies clashed at Saylor's Creek, with Lee suffering heavy losses. Lee tried to retreat westward to escape Grant's pursuing army, but Lee's movement was blocked by a Union cavalry unit commanded by General Philip Sheridan. Trapped by Union armies and reduced now to less than thirty thousand men, Lee knew that further battle and bloodshed were senseless; he could never defeat Grant's larger and better-equipped force. Lee sent word to Grant that he was willing to discuss terms of surrender.

On April 9, the two great battle-weary generals met at Appomattox Courthouse to discuss surrender terms. Remembering the phrase "with malice toward none" from Lincoln's Second Inaugural Address, Grant imposed charitable terms of surrender upon Lee. Lee's troops would simply lay down their weapons and promise to go home and fight no more. Confederate soldiers could keep their horses and mules, which would be needed for spring plowing and planting. Lee's men were hungry, and Grant ordered rations for twenty-five thousand men to be sent to Lee's army.

The next day, Lee's men formally surrendered, laying down their weapons and battle flags before the victorious Union army. A few more Confederate regiments outside of Virginia fought on sporadically for a few weeks. But with Lee's surrender, the great civil war to restore the Union and end slavery was essentially over.

Reconstructing the Nation

More than 600,000 Americans lost their lives during the Civil War. Thousands more were permanently or partially disabled. Throughout the South, cities, towns, farms, homes, railroads, and roads were damaged and destroyed. The region's economy was in shambles. Without slave labor, the great Southern plantations would be unable to operate profitably. Moreover, even though the battle was over, the hostile feelings between Northerners and Southerners continued. When Lee surrendered to Grant at Appomattox Courthouse, the United States was still a house bitterly divided.

Lincoln knew that he faced a formidable task in reconstructing his fragmented nation. But even before Lee surrendered, Lincoln had been planning for the day when his nation would be fully restored. On April 11, 1865, Lincoln delivered a speech on reconstruction in Washington, D.C. He rejected the idea put forth by some Northern-

The ruins of a Confederate arsenal in Richmond, Virginia. Southern cities, towns, farms, and homes were ravaged by the Civil War, and more than 600,000 Americans on both sides were killed.

ers that the rebellious Southern states should not be quickly readmitted to the Union. "Let us all join in doing the acts necessary to restoring the proper practical relations between these states and the Union,"[36] said Lincoln. He applauded the voters of Louisiana, who passed a resolution swearing allegiance to the Union and adopting a new state constitution that prohibited slavery.

Lincoln's plan to reconstruct the Union involved keeping Union armies in force in the South to maintain order and to protect the rights of newly freed slaves. Lincoln also planned to extend full citizenship rights to most Southerners, including those who served in the Confederate army, as long as they took an oath of allegiance to the Union. But Lincoln believed that those who had held high positions in the Confederate government and those who had served as officers in its army should not be able to vote or hold public office in the reconstructed United States. Most importantly, the state governments of the rebellious South must accept the Emancipation Proclamation. Slavery would have to be one of the casualties of the Civil War.

Lincoln also had formed a plan to deal with the hundreds of thousands of Southern slaves who had been liberated during the war. By the war's end, many were working for the U.S. government as soldiers or laborers. The federal government had begun to set up farms

The Freedmen's Bureau

In March 1865, Congress, with President Lincoln's approval, established the Bureau of Refugees, Freedmen, and Abandoned Lands to deal with the overwhelming problems faced by slaves who had suddenly been set free. Many of these former slaves knew only life on their plantations. Now they were on their own; they were required to find homes and work to support themselves and their families. The Freedmen's Bureau attempted to help these former slaves as they took their first steps toward personal and financial independence by providing food, shelter, clothing, and medical care.

At first, the Freedmen's Bureau attempted to employ freed slaves on large Southern plantations that the U.S. government had confiscated during the Civil War. This plan worked only for a short time because most of these confiscated lands were eventually returned to their owners.

The most successful initiative of the Freedmen's Bureau was its educational program. The bureau established close to three thousand schools throughout the South, teaching freed slaves and their children how to read, write, and compute. Most former slaves were illiterate. The bureau also founded several black colleges, including Howard University in Washington, D.C.

throughout the ravished South, and Lincoln hoped that freed slaves could work on these farms for fair wages. He also wanted to extend freed slaves the right to vote and hold public office.

Amending the Constitution

For Lincoln, permanently resolving the issue of slavery was the key to reconstructing the United States. He knew that his Emancipation Proclamation was solely a wartime measure advanced to cripple the South's ability to continue the war. Lincoln feared that sometime in the future the Supreme Court or Congress might invalidate the Emancipation, which Lincoln had sworn never to retract or modify. The only way to block a reversal of the Emancipation Proclamation was to draft a constitutional amendment to outlaw slavery forever.

As early as 1862, Republicans in Congress, with Lincoln's approval, began drafting a constitutional amendment to abolish slavery. In April 1864, the Thirteenth Amendment to the Constitution was formally introduced as a measure to be voted upon in the U.S. Senate.

The Republican-dominated Senate passed the amendment by the required two-thirds vote, but to become law, the amendment would also have to be approved by two-thirds of the House of Representatives and three-quarters of the state legislatures as well. In June, the amendment abolishing slavery came to a vote in the House. House Democrats voted against the amendment, however, and it failed to garner the required two-thirds vote.

Republicans kept the issue alive. In the election of 1864, many Republican candidates campaigned on a platform that included ratification of the Thirteenth Amendment. Lincoln's reelection signaled that the amendment would eventually become law. The Republicans enjoyed some gains in the House of Representatives in the election, and these newly elected congressmen were anxious to kill slavery by making its prohibition part of the Constitution.

On January 31, 1865, even before the new congressmen took office, the Thirteenth Amendment again came to a vote in the House of Representatives. Lincoln had pressured Democratic congressmen who were leaving office to listen to the will of the American people and endorse the amendment. Some of these congressmen listened to Lincoln. This time, the measure attracted more than the required two-thirds of the vote.

Passage of the Thirteenth Amendment

Abolitionists cheered the House vote. Nonetheless, the Thirteenth Amendment was not yet a part of the Constitution. Having passed the Senate and House of Representatives, the Thirteenth Amendment still needed to be ratified by three-quarters of the individual state legislatures. Since Lincoln had maintained throughout the war that the South had never legally seceded from the Union, several Southern states would have to endorse the Thirteenth Amendment for it to achieve the required three-fourths of state legislatures.

The states began to act immediately. Within two months, the Thirteenth Amendment was approved by nineteen state legislatures, including Louisiana and Arkansas, which, near the end of the war, pledged allegiance to the Union and passed new state constitutions that outlawed slavery. As of April 1865, however, the Thirteenth Amendment still needed to be ratified by three more states. The Civil War was over, but the slaves were not yet officially free. Their freedom depended on the untested legality of the Emancipation Proclamation; the abolition of slavery was not yet a part of the Constitution.

But Lincoln would not live to see the passage of the Thirteenth Amendment. In April 1865, just days after Lee's surrender to Grant marked the end of the Civil War, Lincoln himself became a casualty of that terrible four-year conflict.

A Theater Outing

On April 14, 1865, Lincoln was in good spirits. The war was virtually over. Several days earlier, Lincoln had visited Richmond. There, as he walked through the streets of the former capital of the Confederacy, freed black people had cheered him as their liberator. Lincoln had not only steered the North to victory, but he had expunged from his nation the great sin of slavery. In Richmond, he had seen firsthand the fruits of victory—the expressions of joy in the faces of free people who had once been slaves.

On the evening of April 14, Lincoln planned an evening of light entertainment with his wife, Mary, an opportunity to escape, for a few hours, the pain of war and the serious work of reconstructing the nation that lie ahead. The president and his wife had planned an outing to Ford's Theatre in Washington to see a performance of a British comedy, *Our American Cousin*. General and Mrs. Grant were supposed to accompany the Lincolns, but the Grants backed out at the last minute. Major Henry Rathbone and his fiancée, Clara Harris, a senator's daughter, attended instead.

The president's party arrived at Ford's Theatre a little late; the play had already begun when they entered the flag-draped presidential box in the theater balcony. When they were seated, the band struck "Hail to the Chief," and the audience applauded. Then the play continued. President and Mrs. Lincoln enjoyed the action on stage, and they laughed heartily at the play's many humorous lines.

John Wilkes Booth was an actor who had often performed in plays seen by the president.

The Assassin Arrives

Also arriving late for the start of the play that evening was an actor well known at Ford's Theatre, John Wilkes Booth. Booth had been a Virginia militiaman before the war; he had been among the guards stationed at the hanging of John Brown in 1859. When the Civil War began, Booth supported the Confederate cause, but he did not join the Confederate army. During the war, he made a good living as an actor. His father, Junius Brutus Booth, and his older brother, Edwin, were also accomplished actors. Lincoln had seen all three Booths perform on Washington's stages.

Lincoln is mortally wounded by Booth in the presidential box at Ford's Theatre. The president died early the next morning.

Booth had come to believe that Lincoln was mainly to blame for the South's troubles at the close of the war. Feeling guilty and cowardly for not having enlisted in the Rebel army, Booth vowed to take some other action to help the South's cause. At first, he planned to kidnap Lincoln and exchange him for several thousand Confederate prisoners of war. On March 17, 1865, Booth and a few accomplices actually attempted a kidnapping of Lincoln on the outskirts of Washington at Soldier's Home, where the Lincolns sometimes spent the night, but the Lincolns were not there that night.

When the war ended, Booth was determined to kill President Lincoln. He planned the assassination with four coconspirators. In one night of terror, Booth hoped to murder Lincoln, Vice President Andrew Johnson, and Secretary of State William Seward. When Booth heard through one of the stagehands at Ford's Theatre that the Lincolns would be attending the performance of *Our American Cousin* on the evening of April 14, he launched his plan.

In the middle of the play, Booth entered the theater and climbed the stairs to the presidential box. The guard watching the rear door of the box was not at his post, and the door was unlocked. Booth was armed with a dagger and loaded derringer pistol. He waited for a moment when the theater audience erupted in laughter and applause, then he slipped into the president's box, fired his pistol at the back of Lincoln's head, and slashed at Colonel Rathbone with the dagger. Before anyone realized what had happened, Booth jumped from the balcony to the stage and shouted something to the audience. Some theatergoers thought he yelled *"Sic semper tyrannis!"*—Virginia's state motto, which meant "Thus be it ever to tyrants." Other witnesses claimed that Booth had shouted "The South is avenged!" With that, Booth quickly fled Ford's Theatre.

The Death of a President

The crowd at Ford's Theatre was stunned. At first, they had no idea why the man wielding a long knife had jumped from the balcony to the stage. Soon, however, there were shouts from the presidential box. President Lincoln had been shot. A call went out for any doctors in the audience.

Two physicians hurried to Lincoln's side. His head was bleeding badly, and he was unconscious. The doctors applied mouth-to-mouth resuscitation to keep the president breathing, but they knew already that their efforts were useless. Booth's bullet had entered Lincoln's head behind his left ear and lodged in his brain behind his right eye. "His wound is mortal," said one of the physicians; "it is impossible for him to recover."[37]

Lincoln was carried out of Ford's Theatre to a house across the street. Attendants placed him in a bed in a rear room. The news of the attempt on Lincoln's life quickly spread through the streets of Washington, and within minutes, Lincoln advisers were hurrying to the scene. Doctors could do nothing for the mortally wounded president; he lay in bed barely breathing. He had been shot on Good Friday. At 7:22 on Saturday morning, his breathing stopped. President Lincoln was dead.

Mourning the Slain President

The entire nation, North and South, was stunned by the assassination of Lincoln. Some bitter Southerners undoubtedly applauded Booth's murderous deed, but most Americans, even those who had criticized Lincoln's wartime policies, mourned his passing. They sensed that a great leader had been taken from them at a time when the war-torn nation needed strong leadership.

A short and simple funeral service was held for Lincoln at the White House on April 19. Then his coffin was transported by wagon to the Capitol building. Leading the funeral procession was a regiment of African American soldiers. The coffin was set in the Capitol's large rotunda room for two days so that visitors could pass through and pay their respects to their fallen president. Thousands of mourners entered the building and silently passed Lincoln's casket, offering prayers and shedding tears as they went by.

The Death of John Wilkes Booth

After shooting President Lincoln at Ford's Theatre, John Wilkes Booth jumped from the presidential box in the balcony to the stage. As he leapt to the stage, Booth stumbled and landed awkwardly, breaking a bone in his shin. After shouting words of defiance at the theater audience, he rushed from the building, mounted his waiting horse, and rode off into the night.

Booth fled for the safety of the Virginia countryside. He found a physician to treat his broken leg. Despite the efforts of Federal troops and bounty hunters—a $50,000 reward was offered for Booth's arrest—he was able to remain at large for almost two weeks. On April 26, a Union cavalry battalion that had been tracking Booth and David Herold, one of his accomplices, caught up to them. They tried to hide in a Virginia tobacco barn, but soldiers surrounded the building and ordered the two fugitives out. When they refused, the soldiers set fire to the barn. Herold surrendered, but Booth remained defiant to the end. He refused to surrender, and he was shot in the head by a Yankee soldier. In his last moments of life, Booth stated, "Tell my mother I died for my country. . . . I did what I thought was best."

Four of Booth's accomplices, including Herold, were tried and found guilty of conspiring to murder Lincoln. They were hanged on July 7, 1865.

Union soldiers set fire to the barn in which John Wilkes Booth hid. Refusing to surrender, Booth was killed by a shot to the head.

Lincoln is mourned in Philadelphia, Pennsylvania. The train carrying Lincoln's body made many such stops on the route to Springfield, Illinois.

On April 21, Lincoln's coffin was loaded onto a train and transported for burial sixteen hundred miles away in Springfield, Illinois. All along the train route, mourners gathered to view the passing train. As the train passed through towns and cities, church bells tolled and soldiers and militiamen lined the tracks to salute their fallen commander.

Lincoln's body was laid to rest in Oak Ridge Cemetery, just outside of Springfield, on May 4. In a sense, he, too, had become a casualty of the great civil war to end slavery. In his Second Inaugural Address, he had predicted that God would not allow the war to end until the nation paid for the sin of slavery, until every drop of blood taken by the slave master's whip was repaid with a drop of blood on the battlefield. Early in his political career, Lincoln had tolerated slavery; in his First Inaugural Address, he had offered the rebellious Southern states the opportunity to return to the Union with slavery still in place. Now, as the war was coming to an end, Lincoln had shed his own blood so that slavery could be abolished.

The Thirteenth Amendment Becomes Law

At the time of Lincoln's death, the Thirteenth Amendment to the Constitution had not yet been ratified by three-quarters of the state legislatures. Final ratification of the amendment finally came on December 18, 1865, eight months after Lincoln's death.

The Thirteenth Amendment consists of two sections, each only one sentence long:

> *Section 1* Neither slavery nor involuntary servitude, except as a punishment for crime whereof the party shall have been duly convicted, shall exist within the United States, or any place subject to their jurisdiction.
>
> *Section 2* Congress shall have the power to enforce this article by appropriate legislation.

In simple language, the amendment gives the force of law to Lincoln's wartime Emancipation Proclamation. Slavery is prohibited throughout the United States and its territories. Only those convicted of crimes and serving prison terms can be made to work against their wills. Slavery was officially abolished from American soil; it would never again return.

The Civil War Amendments

The Constitution was twice more amended in the wake of the Civil War. The Thirteenth, Fourteenth, and Fifteenth Amendments to the Constitution are often called the "Civil War amendments" because they were passed as a result of the war. All three amendments concern the civil rights of African American citizens who were formerly slaves.

Soon after the passage of the Thirteenth Amendment, it became clear that the South's freed slaves were not totally free. They were legally free from their former owners, but they were not free to enjoy all the rights of American citizenship—the right to vote and hold public office, to serve on a jury, to live in the neighborhood of choice, to compete fairly in the job market, or to enjoy social amenities such as parks, restaurants, and hotels. Particularly in the South, freed slaves lived as second-class citizens, unable to enjoy the freedoms taken for granted by white Americans. Recognizing these conditions, Congress, in 1867, acted by proposing the Fourteenth Amendment to the Constitution.

The heart of the Fourteenth Amendment is the so-called equal protection clause in its first section. That section guarantees that all people born in the United States are citizens of the United States and citizens of the state in which they reside. It also guarantees that all citizens will be treated equally under the law:

> No State shall make or enforce any law which shall abridge the privileges or immunities of citizens of the United States; nor shall any State deprive any person of life, liberty, or property, without due process of law; nor deny to any person within its jurisdiction the equal protection of the laws.

This amendment attempted to ensure that all American citizens, regardless of race, would enjoy all the rights and privileges of U.S. citizens. Thus, under the law, freed slaves and their children must receive fair and equal treatment.

The members of the Republican-controlled Congress knew that getting Southern states to ratify the Fourteenth Amendment would be difficult. Therefore, they refused to allow the states of the former Confederacy to seat their representatives in Congress until those states ratified the amendment. The amendment was eventually approved by both the Senate and House of Representatives and by three-quarters of the state legislatures. It became a part of the Constitution on July 28, 1868.

The Right to Vote

In 1870, Congress again acted on behalf of African American citizens when it became clear that Southern states were barring blacks from voting. In the South, laws were passed making it illegal for ex-slaves, their children, or grandchildren to vote. The Fifteenth Amendment was proposed to remedy this situation. Like the Thirteenth Amendment, the Fifteenth contains two sections, each a single sentence in length:

> *Section 1* The right of citizens of the United States to vote shall not be denied or abridged by the United States or by any State on account of race, color, or previous condition of servitude.

Section 2 The Congress shall have power to enforce this article by appropriate legislation.

The Fifteenth Amendment became part of the Constitution on March 30, 1870.

The intent of the three Civil War amendments was to free the slaves forever and to guarantee to them and their descendants all the rights

The Impeachment of President Johnson

Immediately after President Lincoln's death, Vice President Andrew Johnson took the oath of office as the seventeenth president of the United States. Johnson, a Southerner, was chosen as Lincoln's running mate for the 1864 election because Republican Party leaders believed that he might attract votes in the slave states that had not seceded from the Union. Lincoln hoped that Johnson, who was born in North Carolina and later settled in Tennessee, might be able to help reconstruct the South and bring it back to the Union after the war.

Soon after his ascension to the presidency, Johnson ran into trouble with the Republican-controlled Congress. He refused to support the Fourteenth Amendment, and he vetoed a bill to establish the Freedmen's Bureau to assist former slaves; both measures had wide support in Congress. In 1866, Congress passed, over Johnson's veto, the Tenure of Office Act, which attempted to limit the president's power to remove federal officials from office. In 1868, when Johnson tried to dismiss and replace Secretary of War Edwin Stanton, the House of Representatives accused the president of high crimes—specifically, violating the Tenure of Office Act—and voted to impeach him, or remove him from office.

The Constitution calls for the Senate to try a president who has been impeached by the House. If two-thirds of the Senate votes for impeachment, the president is removed from office. In this case, the Senate failed by a single vote to remove Johnson from office. He was allowed to serve the remainder of his term.

Johnson was the first U.S. president to be subjected to the impeachment process. In 1972, a House of Representatives committee voted to impeach President Richard Nixon for obstructing the investigation of a break-in at the Democratic Party's campaign headquarters at Washington's Watergate Hotel. Rather than face impeachment, Nixon resigned from office.

A *poster celebrates the Fifteenth Amendment to the Constitution. This amendment guaranteed every American citizen the right to vote regardless of race, color, or previous condition of servitude.*

and privileges of American citizenship, including the right to vote. These measures, passed within five years of the end of the Civil War, were an attempt to prevent the United States from remaining a house divided along racial lines. By passing these three amendments, Congress and the state legislatures were certainly acting in accordance with Lincoln's wishes. At Gettysburg, he had predicted "a new birth of freedom" for his country, and in his Second Inaugural Address, he had hoped for "a just, and a lasting peace" for his war-torn nation. These Civil War amendments attempted to re-create the United States as a nation of free and equal citizens.

The Legacy of the Emancipation Proclamation

On August 28, 1963, more than one hundred years after Abraham Lincoln issued his Emancipation Proclamation, Martin Luther King Jr., a young African American civil rights leader born in Atlanta, Georgia, in 1929, delivered a stirring speech before a crowd of more than 200,000 people gathered in front of the Lincoln Memorial in Washington, D.C. King began his speech—later called "I Have a Dream"—by reminding his audience, in Lincolnesque language, that a century had passed since Lincoln set the slaves free:

> Fivescore years ago, a great American in whose symbolic shadow we stand today, signed the Emancipation Proclamation. The momentous decree came as a great beacon light of

Martin Luther King Jr. speaks to a crowd of more than 200,000 people in front of the Lincoln Memorial in August 1963. His "I Have a Dream" speech began with words that echoed Lincoln's Gettysburg Address of one hundred years before.

hope to millions of Negro slaves who had been seared in the flames of withering injustice. It came as a joyous daybreak to end the long night of their captivity.

Then King went on to assert that one hundred years after Lincoln's dramatic act, "the Negro still is not free." He is "still sadly crippled by the manacles of segregation and the chains of discrimination"; he lives "on a lonely island of poverty in the midst of a vast ocean of material prosperity"; he "is still languished in the corners of American society and finds himself in exile in his own land." According to King, the promise of freedom put forth in Lincoln's Emancipation Proclamation was a promissory note on which America has defaulted, "a bad check . . . which has come back marked 'insufficient funds.'"[38]

Did the Emancipation Proclamation, as King suggests, end slavery but, in some sense, fail to free the African American people? Why, according to King, were America's black citizens still not free in 1963, a century after the issuance of the Emancipation Proclamation and the passage of the Thirteenth, Fourteenth, and Fifteenth Amendments to the U.S. Constitution—measures specifically designed to extend all the rights and privileges of American citizenship to the freed slaves and their descendants?

The Era of Jim Crow

Despite the passage of the Civil War amendments, the South acted swiftly to block the federal government's attempt to extend the rights of citizenship to freed slaves. State legislatures passed laws, known as "Black Codes," to restrict the freedom of African American citizens. Homeless former slaves were arrested and fined heavily for vagrancy, then sent to a white person's plantation to work off their fines. Freed slaves were forced to purchase expensive licenses to apply for jobs. African Americans who committed minor crimes were given stiff prison sentences.

Eventually the so-called Jim Crow laws—named after a character who often appeared in African American minstrel shows—were enacted to restrict the social and political rights of black citizens of the South. Blacks were prohibited from frequenting hotels and restaurants patronized by white people. Black children were blocked from enrolling in public schools established for white students. Doctors and hospitals refused to treat black patients, even in emergencies. Laws were also passed to prevent black citizens from voting. A voting fee, called a poll tax, which few blacks could afford to pay, was imposed in many Southern states. "Grandfather clauses"—laws that prohibited anyone whose grandparents were slaves from voting—were also enacted to prevent black citizens from going to the polls. Blacks were also prohibited by law from serving on juries.

These Black Codes and Jim Crow laws certainly violated the spirit of the Fourteenth and Fifteenth Amendments. The federal government, however, turned its head when the southern states began passing legislation designed to segregate African American citizens. An unwritten compromise between the federal government and the South allowed the Southern states to deal with their African American citizens as they wished as long as those states returned to the Union and publicly accepted the Civil War amendments.

The Case of *Plessy v. Ferguson*

The Supreme Court essentially approved the South's attempt to ignore the Fourteenth Amendment in its decision in the case of *Plessy v. Ferguson,* which concerned a piece of Jim Crow legislation in Louisiana. The Louisiana Railway Accommodations Act, passed in 1890, required all railroad companies operating within the state to provide separate accommodations for white and black passengers. Any passenger entering a railroad car not designated for his or her race would be subjected to a fine of $25.

On June 7, 1892, Homer Plessy, a man who was one-eighth black and seven-eighths white but still considered a Negro under Louisiana law, boarded a train in New Orleans and found a seat in the car reserved for white passengers. The railroad's detective arrested Plessy. He was brought to the Criminal District Court of New Orleans, where he was tried and found guilty by Judge John Ferguson of violating the Railway Accommodations Act. Citing the equal protection clause of the Fourteenth Amendment, Plessy appealed his conviction to the U.S. Supreme Court. He believed that he had not been granted equal protection of the law.

On May 6, 1896, the Supreme Court voted 7–1 to uphold Plessy's conviction. The Court's decision, delivered by Associate Justice Henry Billings Brown, stated that the Fourteenth Amendment "could not have been intended to abolish distinctions based upon color, or to enforce social, as distinguished from political equality, or a commingling of the two races upon terms unsatisfactory to either."[39] In other words, the state of Louisiana was allowed to separate citizens according to race in social situations. The ruling began a policy later known as "separate but equal": A law could mandate separate public facilities for white and black citizens, as long as those facilities were of essentially equal quality.

Thus, the Supreme Court gave its stamp of approval to all Jim Crow legislation. Indeed, during the years following the *Plessy* decision, Southern states and communities imposed additional Jim Crow legislation. Parks, golf courses, barbershops and beauty parlors, sports arenas, movie theaters, restaurants, and hotels became rigidly segregated throughout the South. But racial segregation was not restricted to the South. In the North, racial segregation was perhaps less overt, but some Northern states segregated schools and set up roadblocks for blacks who wanted to integrate white neighborhoods and workplaces.

The *Plessy* decision insured that Jim Crow would remain firmly in place for more than fifty years. Four decades into the twentieth century, the United States was still a house divided, though not, as in Lincoln's time, half slave and half free. The United States was a nation divided along racial lines, with legal, political, and social barriers that rigidly separated white and black citizens.

The Civil Rights Movement

The end of World War II, however, brought the promise of positive change for African American citizens. During the war, the United States had helped defeat the racist regime of Adolf Hitler, who had ordered the imprisonment and execution of European Jews, Slavs,

Southern Jim Crow laws prohibited black and white children from attending the same schools.

The Voices of Former Slaves

During the 1930s, the Federal Writers' Project, a program funded by the Works Progress Administration that employed researchers and writers to create thousands of publications centered on American themes, embarked on an ambitious project to record the lives of former slaves. Federal Writers' Project researchers interviewed about two thousand former slaves, resulting in an extensive collection of forty-one volumes that provided readers and researchers with a first-hand view of life under slavery.

Some former slaves told harrowing stories of their time in captivity. For example, Mary Reynolds, a Louisiana slave who was one hundred years old when interviewed, called life under slavery "the worst days ever seed in the world. They was the things past telling, but I got the scars on my old body to show to this day." She described fellow slaves stripped naked, placed in stocks, and beaten with a whip by the slave overseer. Jenny Proctor, a Texas slave, describes being sent out to the cotton fields at age ten to engage in hard labor.

Not all slaves had negative memories of their lives in bondage, however. Harriet McFarlin Payne describes living in a neat cabin, wearing good clothing, and having plenty to eat. "If all slaves had belonged to white folks like ours, there wouldn't been any freedom wanted," she told Federal Writers' Project interviewers.

Some of the interviews contained in this forty-one-volume oral history project also appear in *Voices from Slavery* by Norman Yetman and in *Lay My Burden Down: A Folk History of Slavery* by B. A. Botkin.

and other people he judged to be ethnically inferior to his so-called master race. Thousands of African American soldiers, sailors, and airmen had fought heroically in the war to defeat Hitler. Now, as these brave veterans returned home, many Americans, both black and white, began to turn a critical eye toward their own nation's racist policies. These citizens began to question how Americans could go to war to defeat Hitler yet still tolerate racial segregation in the United States.

Soon after the war ended in 1945, some of the rigid barriers that separated the races in the United States began to fall. In August 1945, a few weeks after the end of the war, the Brooklyn Dodgers baseball team signed a young player named Jackie Robinson, a star of the Kansas City Monarchs of the Negro leagues. Robinson played for the

Dodgers' minor league teams for two seasons, then made his major league debut in April 1947. He became the first African American to play major league baseball in the twentieth century. Robinson excelled on the field, and soon other teams were signing talented African American players. Major league baseball, which had been reserved for whites only since the time of *Plessy v. Ferguson,* began to integrate.

A year after Robinson's major league debut, President Harry Truman issued an executive order to integrate the U.S. armed forces. Prior to that time, the American armed forces operated separate regiments for white and black soldiers, sailors, and airmen. Truman's order signaled a great change in America's racial climate. The nation was experiencing the beginnings of a great civil rights movement, the first since the passage of the Civil War amendments.

Brown v. Board of Education of Topeka, Kansas

The single event that ignited the civil rights movement was a Supreme Court decision in a school desegregation case. During the late 1940s and early 1950s, the National Association for the Advancement of Colored People (NAACP) began to challenge in court some of the laws that segregated public schools along racial lines. NAACP attorneys argued that forcing black children to attend a school separate from white children denied the black children's Fourteenth Amendment rights to equal protection under the law. Moreover, the attorneys tried to demonstrate in court that the separate schools established for black children were not of equal quality to the schools for whites.

In 1952, the Supreme Court heard four separate school segregation lawsuits under the umbrella title *Brown v. Board of Education of Topeka, Kansas.* After eighteen months of courtroom hearings and deliberations, the Court decided, on May 17, 1954, that "in the field of public education the doctrine of 'separate but equal' has no place. Separate educational facilities are inherently unequal"; black schoolchildren forced to attend separate schools are "deprived of the equal protection of the laws guaranteed by the Fourteenth Amendment."[40]

The Supreme Court's decision in the *Brown* case concerned only public educational facilities, but soon lower courts began using the Court's ruling in that case to invalidate Jim Crow laws that segregated other public facilities—beaches, golf courses, parks. In *Brown,* the budding American civil rights movement now had a solid legal foundation.

Martin Luther King Jr.

In 1955, Martin Luther King Jr. emerged as the leader of the civil rights movement when he led the effort to desegregate municipal

In 1954 the Supreme Court ruled in Brown v. Board of Education *that "separate but equal" public school facilities were in fact inherently unequal. Schools and eventually other public areas were desegregated by law.*

buses in Montgomery, Alabama. Prior to 1955, Montgomery's buses were rigidly segregated: White passengers could sit in the front rows, while black passengers were compelled by law to sit in the back of the bus. If the white section of the bus were full and a white passenger boarded, the black passengers in the first row of seats designated for blacks would have to surrender their seats. On December 1, 1955, a black seamstress, Rosa Parks, refused to surrender her seat to a white passenger. She was fined $14 for breaking the bus segregation law.

Immediately, Montgomery's African American community leaders took action, forming the Montgomery Improvement Association with the twenty-six-year-old King as its leader. King, the minister of Montgomery's Dexter Avenue Baptist Church, ordered a boycott of Montgomery's buses by black citizens. For more than a year, black citizens of Montgomery refused to ride the city buses. On December 20,

King participates in the March on Washington for Jobs and Freedom on August 23, 1963. Later that day he gave his "I Have a Dream" speech.

1956, city officials received a directive from the Supreme Court: Montgomery's bus segregation law was unconstitutional, a violation of the equal protection clause of the Fourteenth Amendment.

King had won a great victory, and he soon took his campaign for civil rights throughout the South. During the next ten years, King helped rip down many of the legal barriers that separated America's white and black citizens. Schools and universities were desegregated. Laws prohibiting blacks from voting were struck down in court. In 1964, the Civil Rights Act was passed, the most important piece of civil rights legislation enacted since the post–Civil War years. The law called for an end to segregation in hotels, restaurants, theaters, sports arenas, and other public commercial facilities. Federal legislation prohibiting discrimination in employment and housing was also passed. In 1965, Congress enacted the Voting Rights Act, which attempted to remove all the barriers that were used to block African American citizens from voting in the South.

King's movement received momentum from several great public marches and public demonstrations. In 1960, a series of restaurant and luncheonette sit-ins by college students throughout the South helped put an end to the practice of prohibiting black citizens from patronizing public eating places. In August 1963, the NAACP and other civil rights organizations planned the March on Washington for Jobs and Freedom, which attracted more than 200,000 protesters to the Lincoln Memorial in Washington. The concluding rally of the march featured King's "I Have a Dream" speech. In March 1965, King led a march from Selma to Montgomery, Alabama, to protest voting restrictions imposed upon Alabama's black citizens.

Free at Last?

King ended his "I Have a Dream" speech with the hope that African American citizens would soon be free:

And when we allow freedom to ring, when we let it ring from every village and hamlet, from every state and city, we will be able to speed up that day when all of God's children— black men and white men, Jews and Gentiles, Catholics and Protestants—will be able to join hands and to sing in the words of the old Negro spiritual, "Free at last, free at last; thank God Almighty, we are free at last."[41]

The Death of Martin Luther King Jr.

Like Abraham Lincoln, Martin Luther King Jr. met an untimely death resulting from an assassin's bullet.

In late March 1968, King traveled to Memphis, Tennessee, to speak out on behalf of the city's sanitation workers, who were engaged in a long and bitter strike. At a rally on the evening of April 3, King addressed his supporters in an eloquent speech that hinted that he had few days left on this earth. "Like anybody, I would like to live a long life. Longevity has its place," said King. "But I'm not concerned about that now. I just want to do God's will. And He's allowed me to go up to the mountain. And I've looked over. And I've seen the promised land. I may not get there with you."

The next day, King was out for some fresh air on the balcony of his hotel room when an assassin's bullet struck him in the neck, killing him almost instantly. The bullet was fired by James Earl Ray, a man associated with racist organizations. It was not the first attempt on King's life. In 1956, during the Montgomery Bus Boycott, King's home in Montgomery was the target of a bomb. Two years later, King was stabbed by a black woman at a book signing in New York City.

Like Lincoln, King died with much of his work left undone, though during his life he witnessed the dismantling of many barriers that segregated the races in the United States.

Crowds gather in front of the Lincoln Memorial and around the Reflecting Pool to hear Martin Luther King Jr. speak.

King fell to an assassin's bullet less than five years after delivering that stirring speech. His work to finally free America's black citizens was not yet completed. But the night before he died, King, speaking at a rally in support of striking sanitation workers in Memphis, Tennessee, promised his audience that African American citizens would soon reach the promised land of freedom. King concluded the speech, which became known as "I See the Promised Land," with that vow:

> I just want to do God's will. And He's allowed me to go up to the mountain. And I've looked over. And I've seen the promised land. I may not get there with you. But I want you to know tonight, that we, as a people, will get to the promised land. And I'm happy, tonight. I'm not worried about anything. I'm not fearing any man. Mine eyes have seen the glory of the coming of the Lord.[42]

Whether America's black citizens have reached that promised land is still a matter of national public debate. Perhaps, more than a century and a quarter after Lincoln's delivery of the Emancipation Proclamation, African Americans have not yet reached the promised land of absolute freedom and equality. Perhaps the effort to guarantee America's black citizens all the rights of American citizenship is a continuing process, which began during the abolitionist movement before the Civil War, gained momentum from Lincoln's Emancipation Proclamation and from the Civil War amendments to the U.S. Constitution, and carried on through the civil rights movement led by King during the 1950s and 1960s. If that is the case, Lincoln's Emancipation Proclamation, issued in 1863, was a vital early step in that process.

Appendix

Document 1: Preliminary Emancipation Proclamation

On September 22, 1862, five days after the Battle of Antietam, Abraham Lincoln issued the Preliminary Emancipation Proclamation. In this document, Lincoln alerted the South that as of January 1, 1863, the slaves in all states in rebellion against the Union would be "forever free." The document had little impact on the South; no state returned to the Union in the face of Lincoln's threat.

BY THE PRESIDENT OF THE UNITED STATES OF AMERICA
A PROCLAMATION.

I, Abraham Lincoln, President of the United States of America, and Commander-in-chief of the Army and Navy thereof, do hereby proclaim and declare that hereafter, as heretofore, the war will be prossecuted for the object of practically restoring the constitutional relation between the United States, and each of the states, and the people thereof, in which states that relation is, or may be suspended, or disturbed.

That it is my purpose, upon the next meeting of Congress to again recommend the adoption of a practical measure tendering pecuniary aid to the free acceptance or rejection of all slave-states, so called, the people whereof may not then be in rebellion against the United States, and which states, may then have voluntarily adopted, or thereafter may voluntarily adopt, immediate, or gradual abolishment of slavery within their respective limits; and that the effort to colonize persons of African descent, with their consent, upon this continent, or elsewhere, with the previously obtained consent of the Governments existing there, will be continued.

That on the first day of January in the year of our Lord, one thousand eight hundred and sixty-three, all persons held as slaves within any state, or designated part of a state, the people whereof shall then be in rebellion against the United States shall be then, thenceforward, and forever free; and the executive government of the United States, including the military and naval authority thereof, will recognize and maintain the freedom of such persons, and will do no act or acts to repress such persons, or any of them, in any efforts they may make for their actual freedom.

That the executive will, on the first day of January aforesaid, by proclamation, designate the States, and parts of states, if any, in which the people thereof respectively, shall then be in rebellion against the United States; and the fact that any state, or the people thereof shall, on that day be, in good faith represented in the Congress of the United States, by members chosen thereto, at elections wherein a majority of the qualified voters of such state shall have participated, shall, in the absence of strong countervailing testimony, be deemed conclusive evidence that such state and the people thereof, are not then in rebellion against the United States.

That attention is hereby called to an act of Congress entitled "An act to make an additional Article of War" approved March 13, 1862, and which act is in the words and figure following:

Be it enacted by the Senate and House of Representatives of the United States of America in Congress assembled, That hereafter the following shall be promulgated as an additional article of war for the government of the army of the United States, and shall be obeyed and observed as such:

Article—. All officers or persons in the military or naval service of the United States are prohibited from employing any of the forces under their respective commands for the purpose of returning fugitives from service or labor, who may have escaped from any persons to whom such service or labor is claimed to be due, and any officer who shall be found guilty by a court-martial of violating this article shall be dismissed from the service.

Sec. 2. *And be it further enacted,* That this act shall take effect from and after its passage.

Also to the ninth and tenth sections of an act entitled "An Act to suppress Insurrection, to punish Treason and Rebellion, to seize and confiscate property of rebels, and for other purposes," approved July 17, 1862, and which sections are in the words and figures following:

Sec. 9. *And be it further enacted,* That all slaves of persons who shall hereafter be engaged in rebellion against the government of the United States, or who shall in any way give aid or comfort thereto, escaping from such persons and taking refuge within the lines of the army; and all slaves captured from such persons or deserted by them and coming under the control of the government of the United States; and all slaves of such persons found *on* (or) being within any place occupied by rebel forces and afterwards occupied by the forces of the United States, shall be deemed captives of war, and shall be forever free of their servitude and not again held as slaves.

SEC. 10. *And be it further enacted,* That no slave escaping into any State, Territory, or the District of Columbia, from any other State, shall be delivered up, or in any way impeded or hindered of his liberty, except for crime, or some offence against the laws, unless the person claiming said fugitive shall first make oath that the person to whom the labor or service of such fugitive is alleged to be due is his lawful owner, and has not borne arms against the United States in the present rebellion, nor in any way given aid and comfort thereto; and no person engaged in the military or naval service of the United States shall, under any pretence whatever, assume to decide on the validity of the claim of any person to the service or labor of any other person, or surrender up any such person to the claimant, on pain of being dismissed from the service.

And I do hereby enjoin upon and order all persons engaged in the military and naval service of the United States to observe, obey, and enforce, within their respective spheres of service, the act, and sections above recited.

And the executive will in due time recommend that all citizens of the United States who shall have remained loyal thereto throughout the rebellion, shall (upon the restoration of the constitutional relation between the United States, and their respective states, and people, if that relation shall have been suspended or disturbed) be compensated for all losses by acts of the United States, including the loss of slaves.

In witness whereof, I have hereunto set my hand, and caused the seal of the United States to be affixed.

Done at the City of Washington, this twenty second day of September, in the year of our Lord, one thousand eight hundred and sixty two, and of the Independence of the United States, the eighty seventh.

ABRAHAM LINCOLN

By the President:
WILLIAM H. SEWARD, Secretary of State.

Document 2: Final Emancipation Proclamation

On January 1, 1863, Abraham Lincoln issued the Final Emancipation Proclamation. This document freed all slaves in states "wherein the people thereof respectively, are this day in rebellion against the United States."

By the President of the United States of America:

A Proclamation.

Whereas, on the twentysecond day of September, in the year of our Lord one thousand eight hundred and sixtytwo, a proclamation was issued by the President of the United States, containing, among other things, the following, towit:

"That on the first day of January, in the year of our Lord one thousand eight hundred and sixty-three, all persons held as slaves within any State or designated part of a State, the people whereof shall then be in rebellion against the United States, shall be then, thenceforward, and forever free; and the Executive Government of the United States, including the military and naval authority thereof, will recognize and maintain the freedom of such persons, and will do no act or acts to repress such persons, or any of them, in any efforts they may make for their actual freedom.

"That the Executive will, on the first day of January aforesaid, by proclamation, designate the States and parts of States, if any, in which the people thereof, respectively, shall then be in rebellion against the United States; and the fact that any State, or the people thereof, shall on that day be, in good faith, represented in the Congress of the United States by members chosen thereto at elections wherein a majority of the qualified voters of such State shall have participated, shall, in the absence of strong countervailing testimony, be deemed conclusive evidence that such State, and the people thereof, are not then in rebellion against the United States."

Now, therefore I, Abraham Lincoln, President of the United States, by virtue of the power in me vested as Commander-in-Chief, of the Army and Navy of the United States in time of actual armed rebellion against the authority and government of the United States, and as a fit and necessary war measure for suppressing said rebellion, do, on this first day of January, in the year of our Lord one thousand eight hundred and sixtythree, and in accordance with my purpose so to do publicly proclaimed for the full period of one hundred days, from the day first above mentioned, order and designate as the States and parts of States wherein the people thereof respectively, are this day in rebellion against the United States, the following, towit:

Arkansas, Texas, Louisiana, (except the Parishes of St. Bernard, Plaquemines, Jefferson, St. Johns, St. Charles, St. James, Ascension, Assumption, Terrebonne, Lafourche, St. Mary, St. Martin, and Orleans, including the City of New-Orleans) Mississippi, Alabama, Florida, Georgia, South-Carolina, North-Carolina, and Virginia, (except the fortyeight counties designated as West Virginia, and also the counties of Berkley, Accomac, Northampton, Elizabeth-City, York, Princess Ann, and Norfolk, including the cities of Norfolk & Portsmouth); and which excepted parts are, for the present, left precisely as if this proclamation were not issued.

And by virtue of the power, and for the purpose aforesaid, I do order and declare that all persons held as slaves within said designated States, and parts of States, are, and henceforward shall be free; and that the Executive government of the United States, including the military and naval authorities thereof, will recognize and maintain the freedom of said persons.

And I hereby enjoin upon the people so declared to be free to abstain from all violence, unless in necessary self-defence; and I recommend to them that, in all cases when allowed, they labor faithfully for reasonable wages.

And I further declare and make known, that such persons of suitable condition, will be received into the armed service of the United States to garrison forts, positions, stations, and other places, and to man vessels of all sorts in said service.

And upon this act, sincerely believed to be an act of justice, warranted by the Constitution, upon military necessity, I invoke the considerate judgment of mankind, and the gracious favor of Almighty God.

In witness whereof, I have hereunto set my hand and caused the seal of the United States to be affixed.

Done at the City of Washington, this first day of January, in the year of our Lord one thousand eight hundred and sixty three, and of the Independence of the United States of America the eighty-seventh.

By the President: ABRAHAM LINCOLN

WILLIAM H. SEWARD, Secretary of State.

Document 3: Gettysburg Address

On November 19, 1863, Abraham Lincoln presented a short speech at the dedication of the national cemetery at Gettysburg, Pennsylvania, where, four months earlier, a great Union battlefield victory had taken place. In this speech, Lincoln, in eloquent words, tried to explain to the people of the United States the reason for this great civil war: It was a war to defend the proposition that all men are created equal.

Address delivered at the dedication of the Cemetery at Gettysburg.

Four score and seven years ago our fathers brought forth on this continent, a new nation, conceived in liberty, and dedicated to the proposition that all men are created equal.

Now we are engaged in a great civil war, testing whether that nation, or any nation so conceived and so dedicated, can long endure. We are met on a great battle-field of that war. We have come to dedicate a portion of that field, as a final resting place for those who here gave their lives that that nation might live. It is altogether fitting and proper that we should do this.

But, in a larger sense, we can not dedicate—we can not consecrate—we can not hallow—this ground. The brave men, living and dead, who struggled here, have consecrated it, far above our poor power to add or detract. The world will little note, nor long remember what we say here, but it can never forget what they did here. It is for us the living, rather, to be dedicated here to the unfinished work which they who fought here have thus far so nobly advanced. It is rather for us to be here dedicated to the great task remaining before us—that from these honored dead we take increased devotion to that cause for which they gave the last full measure of devotion—that we here highly resolve that these dead shall not have died in vain—that this nation, under God, shall have a new birth of freedom—and that government of the people, by the people, for the people, shall not perish from the earth.
November 19. 1863.

Document 4: Second Inaugural Address

On March 4, 1865, Abraham Lincoln delivered his Second Inaugural Address. In this speech, delivered less than six weeks before his death, Lincoln clearly identified slavery as the cause of the Civil War and offered hope that his war-torn nation would be reunited to enjoy a lasting peace.

Fellow Countrymen:

At this second appearing to take the oath of the presidential office, there is less occasion for an extended address than there was at the first. Then a statement, somewhat in detail, of a course to be pursued, seemed fitting and proper. Now, at the expiration of four years, during which public declarations have been constantly called forth on every point and phase of the great contest which still absorbs the attention, and engrosses the energies of the nation, little that is new could be presented. The progress of our arms, upon which all else chiefly depends, is as well known to the public as to myself; and it is, I trust, reasonably satisfactory and encouraging to all. With high hope for the future, no prediction in regard to it is ventured.

On the occasion corresponding to this four years ago, all thoughts were anxiously directed to an impending civil-war. All dreaded it—all sought to avert it. While the inaugeral address was being delivered from this place, devoted altogether to *saving* the Union without war, insurgent agents were in the city seeking to *destroy* it without war—seeking to dissolve the Union, and divide effects, by negotiation. Both parties deprecated war; but one of them would *make* war rather than let the nation survive; and the other would *accept* war rather than let it perish. And the war came.

One eighth of the whole population were colored slaves, not distributed generally over the Union, but localized in the Southern part of it. These slaves constituted a peculiar and powerful interest. All knew that this interest was, somehow, the cause of the war. To strengthen, perpetuate, and extend this interest was the object for which the insurgents would rend the Union, even by war; while the government claimed no right to do more than to restrict the territorial enlargement of it. Neither party expected for the war, the magnitude, or the duration, which it has already attained. Neither anticipated that the *cause* of the conflict might cease with, or even before, the conflict itself should cease. Each looked for an easier triumph, and a result less fundamental and astounding. Both read the same Bible, and pray to the same God; and each invokes His aid against the other. It may seem strange that any men should dare to ask a just God's assistance in wringing their bread from the sweat of other men's faces; but let us judge not that we be not judged. The prayers of both could not be answered; that of neither has been answered fully. The Almighty has His own purposes.

"Woe unto the world because of offences! for it must needs be that offences come; but woe to that man by whom the offence cometh!" If we shall suppose that American Slavery is one of those offences which, in the providence of God, must needs come, but which, having continued through His appointed time, He now wills to remove, and that He gives to both North and South, this terrible war, as the woe due to those by whom the offence came, shall we discern therein any departure from those divine attributes which the believers in a Living God always ascribe to Him? Fondly do we hope—fervently do we pray—that this mighty scourge of war may speedily pass away. Yet, if God wills that it continue, until all the wealth piled by the bond-man's two hundred and fifty years of unrequited toil shall be sunk, and unto every drop of blood drawn with the lash, shall be paid by another drawn with the sword, as was said three thousand years ago, so still it must be said "the judgments of the Lord, are true and righteous altogether."

With malice toward none; with charity for all; with firmness in the right, as God gives us to see the right, let us strive on to finish the work we are in; to bind up the nation's wounds; to care for him who shall have borne the battle, and for his widow, and his orphan—to do all which may achieve and cherish a just, and a lasting peace, among ourselves, and with all nations.

Source Notes

Introduction: The Document That Ended American Slavery

1. Abraham Lincoln, *Selected Speeches and Writings*. New York: Vintage Books, 1992, p. 369.

Chapter 1: Slavery in America

2. Quoted in Philip S. Foner, ed., *The Basic Writings of Thomas Jefferson*. Garden City, NY: Halcyon House, 1950, p. 24.

3. Quoted in Catherine Drinker Bowen, *Miracle at Philadelphia: The Story of the Constitutional Convention*. New York: Book-of-the-Month Club, 1986, p. 47.

4. Quoted in Foner, *The Basic Writings of Thomas Jefferson*, p. 767.

5. Quoted in Diane Ravitch, ed., *The American Reader: Words That Moved a Nation*. New York: HarperCollins, 1990, p. 100.

6. Quoted in George M. Frerickson, ed., *William Lloyd Garrison*. Englewood Cliffs, NJ: Prentice-Hall, 1968, p. 23.

7. Henry David Thoreau, *Civil Disobedience and Other Essays*. New York: Dover Publications, 1993, p. 23.

8. Quoted in William Dudley, ed. *Slavery: Opposing Viewpoints*. San Diego, CA: Greenhaven Press, 1992, pp. 232–34.

9. Quoted in Dudley, *Slavery*, pp. 236–37.

10. Lincoln, *Selected Speeches and Writings*, p. 221.

11. Thoreau, *Civil Disobedience and Other Essays*, p. 40.

Chapter 2: The Draftsman and His Document

12. Lincoln, *Selected Speeches and Writings*, p. 28.

13. Lincoln, *Selected Speeches and Writings*, p. 94.

14. Lincoln, *Selected Speeches and Writings*, p. 131.

15. Lincoln, *Selected Speeches and Writings*, pp. 152, 184.

16. Lincoln, *Selected Speeches and Writings*, pp. 149, 173.

17. Stephen B. Oates, *Abraham Lincoln: The Man Behind the Myths*. New York: Harper & Row, 1984, p. 72.

18. Lincoln, *Selected Speeches and Writings*, pp. 282–83.

19. Lincoln, *Selected Speeches and Writings*, pp. 284–93.

20. Quoted in Oates, *Abraham Lincoln*, p. 98.

21. Quoted in James M. McPherson, *Battle Cry of Freedom: The Civil War Era*. New York: Oxford University Press, 1988, p. 502.

22. Lincoln, *Selected Speeches and Writings*, p. 343.

23. Lincoln, *Selected Speeches and Writings*, p. 345.

24. Lincoln, *Selected Speeches and Writings*, p. 368.

25. Lincoln, *Selected Speeches and Writings*, p. 369.

26. Lincoln, *Selected Speeches and Writings*, p. 369.

27. Quoted in Oates, *Abraham Lincoln*, p. 18.

Chapter 3: The War to Free the Slaves

28. Lincoln, *Selected Speeches and Writings*, p. 386.

29. Lincoln, *Selected Speeches and Writings*, p. 405.

30. Lincoln, *Selected Speeches and Writings*, p. 405.

31. Garry Wills, *Lincoln at Gettysburg: The Words That Remade America*. New York: Simon & Schuster, 1992, p. 89.

32. Lincoln, *Selected Speeches and Writings*, p. 436.

33. Lincoln, *Selected Speeches and Writings*, p. 449.

34. Lincoln, *Selected Speeches and Writings*, p. 450.

35. Lincoln, *Selected Speeches and Writings*, p. 450.

Chapter 4: From Proclamation to Amendment

36. Lincoln, *Selected Speeches and Writings*, p. 456.

37. Quoted in Stephen B. Oates, *With Malice Toward None: The Life of Abraham Lincoln*. New York: Harper & Row, 1977, p. 432.

Chapter 5: The Legacy of the Emancipation Proclamation

38. Martin Luther King Jr., *I Have a Dream: Writings and Speeches That Changed the World*. San Francisco: HarperSanFrancisco, 1992, p. 102.

39. Quoted in Richard Kluger, *Simple Justice: The History of Brown v. Board of Education and Black America's Struggle for Equality*. New York: Alfred A. Knopf, 1976, p. 74.

40. Quoted in Kluger, *Simple Justice,* p. 782.

41. King, *I Have a Dream,* pp. 105–106.

42. King, *I Have a Dream,* p. 203.

For Further Reading

Stephen B. Oates, *The Approaching Fury: Voices of the Storm, 1820–1861*. New York: Harper & Row, 1970. Using first-person narration, Oates allows thirteen key figures, including Abraham Lincoln, to recount the events of the decade preceding the start of the Civil War.

_____, *Our Fiery Trial: Abraham Lincoln, John Brown, and the Civil War Era*. Amherst: University of Massachusetts Press, 1979. This history of the pre–Civil War era focuses on the activities of John Brown and Abraham Lincoln as the United States headed toward civil war.

Arthur H. Shaw, ed., *The Lincoln Encyclopedia*. New York: Macmillan, 1950. This collection of Lincoln's speeches and writings is indexed for easy reference.

Geoffrey C. Ward, Ric Burns, and Ken Burns, *The Civil War: An Illustrated History*. New York: Alfred A. Knopf, 1990. This history of the Civil War, based on the award-winning documentary film, takes readers, through text, illustrations, and interviews, from the arrival of America's first slaves through the conclusion of the Civil War.

Sanford Wexler, *The Civil Rights Movement: An Eyewitness History*. New York: Facts On File, 1993. This illustrated history of the struggle for racial equality in the United States commences with the Emancipation Proclamation and extends through the 1960s; each chapter contains a chronicle of events and eyewitness testimonies.

Works Consulted

Catherine Drinker Bowen, *Miracle at Philadelphia: The Story of the Constitutional Convention.* New York: Book-of-the-Month Club, 1986. This detailed history of the writing of the Philadelphia Convention of 1787 includes discussions of how the framers of the U.S. Constitution dealt with the issue of slavery.

William Dudley, ed., *Slavery: Opposing Viewpoints.* San Diego, CA: Greenhaven Press, 1992. This collection of documents on slavery provides the arguments of both the institution's defenders and those dedicated to its abolition.

Philip S. Foner, ed., *The Basic Writings of Thomas Jefferson.* Garden City, NY: Halcyon House, 1950. This collection of Jefferson's writings contains both the first and final drafts of the Declaration of Independence.

George M. Frerickson, ed., *William Lloyd Garrison.* Englewood Cliffs, NJ: Prentice-Hall, 1968. This anthology offers a collection of some of Garrison's most important writings, including several pieces from the *Liberator.*

Martin Luther King Jr., *I Have a Dream: Writings and Speeches That Changed the World.* San Francisco: HarperSanFrancisco, 1992. This volume contains King's most important speeches and writings.

Richard Kluger, *Simple Justice: The History of Brown v. Board of Education and Black America's Struggle for Equality.* New York: Alfred A. Knopf, 1976. This study of the *Brown v. Board of Education* case offers a detailed history of the movement for civil rights from the Civil War through the 1950s.

Abraham Lincoln, *Selected Speeches and Writings.* New York: Vintage Books, 1992. This single-volume collection contains Lincoln's most important speeches and writings.

James M. McPherson, *Battle Cry of Freedom: The Civil War Era.* New York: Oxford University Press, 1988. McPherson's text details the period of American history from the 1850s through the Civil War.

Stephen B. Oates, *Abraham Lincoln: The Man Behind the Myths.* New York: Harper & Row, 1984. In this study of Lincoln, Oates examines some of the myths surrounding Lincoln; it includes a detailed discussion of his evolving attitudes on slavery and civil rights.

————, *With Malice Toward None: The Life of Abraham Lincoln.* New York: Harper & Row, 1977. This volume is a detailed biography of Lincoln.

Diane Ravitch, ed., *The American Reader: Words That Moved a Nation.* New York: HarperCollins, 1990. This anthology collects key American texts, including several associated with the abolitionist movement and the Civil War.

Henry David Thoreau, *Civil Disobedience and Other Essays.* New York: Dover Publications, 1993. This collection of Thoreau's essays contains "Slavery in Massachusetts" and "A Plea for Captain John Brown."

Garry Wills, *Lincoln at Gettysburg: The Words That Remade America.* New York: Simon & Schuster, 1992. Wills's book offers a detailed textual and cultural analysis of the Gettysburg Address.

Index

Picture Credits

Cover photo: North Wind Picture Archives
Archive Photos, 9, 18, 21
The Bettmann Archive, 12
Corbis-Bettmann, 28
Courtesy New York Historical Society/*Dictionary of American Portraits*, Dover Publications, Inc., 1967, 24
Daguerreotype by Mathew Brady, Courtesy Library of Congress/ *Dictionary of American Portraits*, Dover Publications, Inc., 1967, 36
Engraved by John C. Buttre from a daguerreotype by Mathew Brady/ *Dictionary of American Portraits*, Dover Publications, Inc., 37
Library of Congress, 10, 13, 19, 31, 34, 35, 40, 41 (bottom), 42, 49, 51, 53, 57, 60, 62, 70, 71, 73, 74, 78, 79, 85, 86, 88
Roy Meredith, *Mr. Lincoln's Camera Man: Mathew B. Brady*, Dover Publications, Inc., 1974, 65
National Archives, 23, 26, 41 (top), 67
North Wind Picture Archives, 46
Schomburg Center for Research in Black Culture, 82

About the Author

James Tackach is the author of *Brown v. Board of Education, The Trial of John Brown,* and young adult biographies of Roy Campanella, Henry Aaron, and James Baldwin. He has also authored *Historic Homes of America, Great American Hotels,* and *Fields of Summer: America's Great Ballparks and the Players Who Triumphed in Them.* His articles have appeared in the *New York Times, Providence Journal, America's Civil War,* and a variety of academic publications. He teaches in the English Department at Roger Williams University, Bristol, Rhode Island, and lives in Narragansett, Rhode Island.